PEARSON

my World
GEOGRAPHY

ProGuide

AUSTRALIA AND THE PACIFIC

D1530925

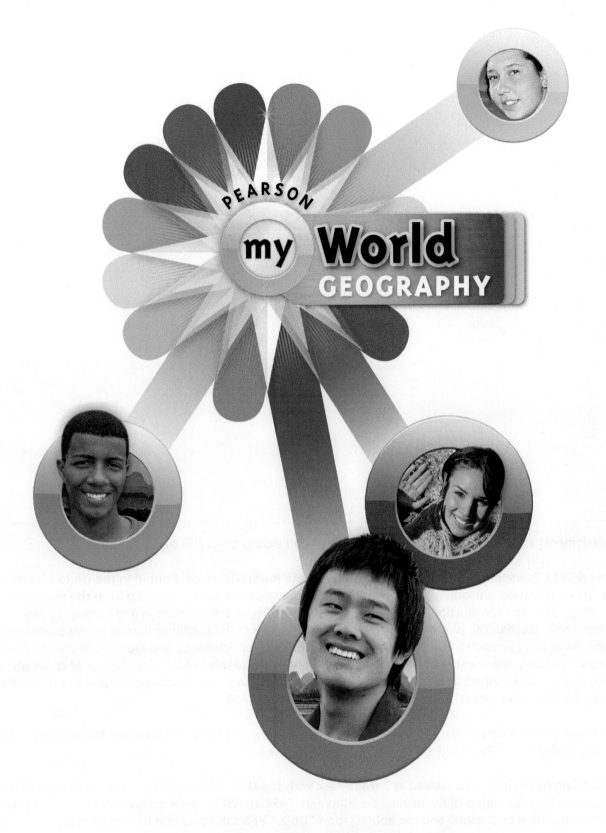

PEARSON

my World
GEOGRAPHY

Australia and the Pacific

PEARSON

Boston, Massachusetts • Chandler, Arizona • Glenview, Illinois • Upper Saddle River, New Jersey

Acknowledgments appear on page T39, which constitutes an extension of this copyright page.

ISBN-13 978-0-13-369589-2
ISBN-10 0-13-369589-1

7 8 9 10 **V064** 14 13 12

Master Teachers and Contributing Authors

George Sabato
Past President, California Council
    for the Social Studies
Placerville Union School District
Placerville, California

Michael Yell
Past President, National Council
    for the Social Studies
Hudson Middle School
Hudson, Wisconsin

Program Authors

Gregory H. Chu
Professor and Chair of Department
    of Geography
University of Wisconsin-La Crosse
La Crosse, Wisconsin

Don Holtgrieve
Department of Planning, Public
    Policy, and Management
University of Oregon
Eugene, Oregon

Susan Hardwick
Department of Geography
University of Oregon
Eugene, Oregon

Program Consultant

Grant Wiggins
President of Authentic Education
Hopewell, New Jersey

Teacher Consultants

James F. Dowd IV
Pasadena, California

Susan M. Keane
Rochester Memorial School
Rochester, Massachusetts

Timothy T. Sprain
Lincoln Middle School
La Crosse, Wisconsin

Marilyn Weiser
North Dakota Geographic
    Alliance Coordinator
Minot State University
Minot, North Dakota

CONTENTS

Australia and the Pacific

How to Read the Table of Contents

- T page numbers refer to teacher resource pages.
- Other page numbers refer to Student Edition pages.
- Follow the first number if your students use the Eastern Hemisphere edition. Follow the second number if your students use the World Geography edition.

Note: Case Studies and Primary Sources Student Edition pages appear only in the [Western/Eastern] edition. Survey users can access these pages online at myworldgeography.com.

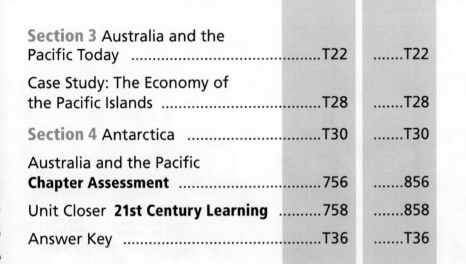

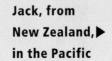

Jack, from
New Zealand, ▶
in the Pacific

Australia and the Pacific

- Prepare to learn about Australia and the Pacific and activate prior knowledge by creating KWL (Know, Want to know, Learned) tables, filling out only the K and W columns. Correct any misconceptions or misinformation on the tables.

- Have students preview maps, photos, and other visuals and predict what they will learn about Australia and the Pacific.

GUIDE ON THE SIDE

What time is it there? Have students look at the time zone display to determine by how many hours the times in Washington, D.C., and Auckland, New Zealand differ. (15 hours)

Analyze Maps Point out the political map and have students answer the following questions.

- What are the capitals of Australia and New Zealand? (Canberra, Wellington)

- How does the size of Australia compare to the rest of the region shown on the map? (It is many times larger than the other countries.)

- How would you describe the majority of countries in the Pacific region? (The majority of countries in the region are made up of very small islands and are often quite isolated from other countries.)

Regional Overview

Australia and the Pacific

Australia, New Zealand, and tens of thousands of other Pacific islands are spread across a vast area of ocean to the south and east of Asia. The people of these islands are as diverse as their geography, which includes high mountains, arid deserts, and icy glaciers.

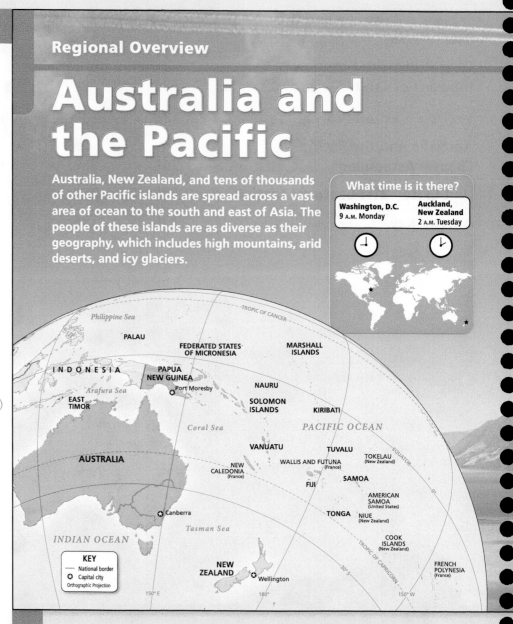

What time is it there?

Washington, D.C.	Auckland, New Zealand
9 A.M. Monday	2 A.M. Tuesday

THE UNIT AHEAD

In this unit, students will

- study the geography of Australia and the Pacific.
- get to know a teenager from New Zealand.
- go On Assignment in Australia and the Pacific.
- make connections between the physical geography, history, politics, and cultures of Australia and the Pacific.

The Unit Ahead

Chapter 24 Australia and the Pacific

my **worldgeography.com**

Plan your trip online by doing a Data Discovery Activity and watching the myStory Video of the region's teen.

my Story

Jack
Age: 17
Home: Auckland, New Zealand
Chapter 24

New Zealand's South Island has many mountains and thick forests.

my Story

Make Predictions Make predictions about the teenage student you will get to know in this unit.

- Jack is 17 years old. How might his life compare to yours? (Sample: He is probably in school and living at home with his parents like me. We might have similar interests, too, like music and sports.)

- Locate New Zealand on the map on the previous page and notice the distance between it and other countries. How do you think this distance might affect Jack's life? (He might be part of a culture that is not found many other places.)

NOTES

GEOGRAPHY

Volcanic Activity Many of the volcanic islands in the Pacific region have active volcanoes, including cone volcanoes (with frequent small or moderate eruptions) and caldera volcanoes (with infrequent moderate or large eruptions). In Vanuatu, the 4,908-foot Aoba volcano has had small eruptions in recent years, although a larger eruption almost 300 years ago destroyed the population of the nearby Nduindui area. In Papua New Guinea, the large Rabaul caldera volcano and smaller cone volcanoes erupt frequently, including in 1994, when an eruption covered the Rabaul township with ash. New Zealand includes six areas known for their volcanic activity, five on North Island and one offshore.

Analyze Visuals Ask students to look at the labeled satellite photo, which shows key physical patterns in the region.

- Where would you expect most people in Australia to settle? Explain. (Sample: Since the interior of the continent is dry, I would expect most of the population to live along the milder coast of the continent.)

- How does the geography of New Zealand appear to vary between North Island and South Island? (South Island appears much more mountainous.)

- Name one geographic challenge the low-lying atolls in the Pacific might constantly face. (Sample: erosion)

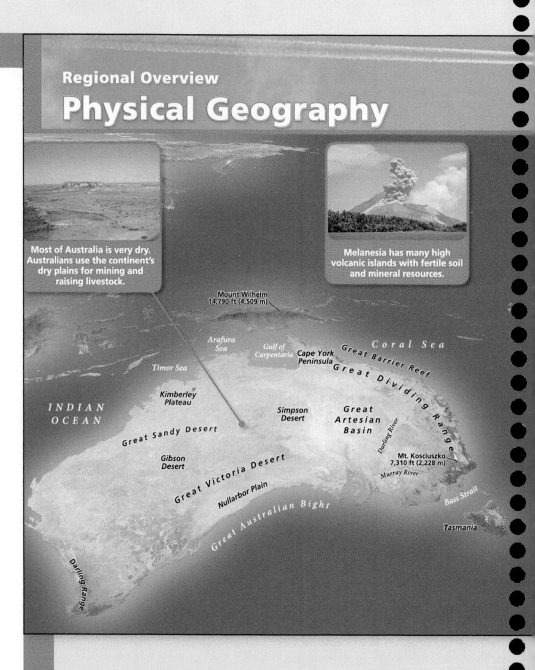

Regional Overview
Physical Geography

Most of Australia is very dry. Australians use the continent's dry plains for mining and raising livestock.

Melanesia has many high volcanic islands with fertile soil and mineral resources.

Mount Wilhelm 14,790 ft (4,509 m)

Arafura Sea

Gulf of Carpentaria

Cape York Peninsula

Coral Sea

Great Barrier Reef

Timor Sea

Great Dividing Range

Kimberley Plateau

INDIAN OCEAN

Simpson Desert

Great Artesian Basin

Darling River

Great Sandy Desert

Mt. Kosciuszko 7,310 ft (2,228 m)

Gibson Desert

Great Victoria Desert

Murray River

Nullarbor Plain

Bass Strait

Great Australian Bight

Tasmania

Darling Range

NOTES

QUICK FACTS

New Zealand's Glaciers New Zealand's Southern Alps are home to about 370 glaciers. The largest is the Tasman Glacier, which flows down the country's famous Mount Cook, or Aoraki. The glacier measured eighteen miles long in 1990, but by 2008 it had shrunk to fourteen miles, with a 4.4-mile-long lake at the glacier's lower end. As the glacier is shrinking, the lake is growing slowly. Scientists believe that as the lake expands, the Tasman Glacier will eventually shrink by up to 2,640 feet a year.

Many Pacific islands are low-lying atolls, islands formed by coral reefs.

PACIFIC OCEAN

North Island

Cook Strait

Aoraki (Mt. Cook)
12,316 ft (3,754 m)

South Island

Southern Alps

New Zealand's Southern Alps are home to more than 20 mountains higher than 10,000 feet.

Regional Flyover

You begin your flight at Easter Island, the easternmost settlement in Polynesia. From here you fly west across the Pacific Ocean, traveling over the thousands of high volcanic islands and low coral atolls that form the Pacific islands. These islands are spread out over 116 million square miles of ocean.

Flying low over the ocean, your airplane reaches Papua New Guinea, a nation on the eastern half of the island of New Guinea. Although it is just south of the Equator, Papua New Guinea has peaks high enough to receive snow. As your plane circles back to the southeast, you fly over New Zealand's icy glaciers, tall mountains, and thick rain forests.

Then you travel west across the Tasman Sea to Australia, following the 1,250-mile-long Great Barrier Reef along Australia's northeast coast. Finally you circle south, landing on the deserts of central Australia. Here you find Uluru, or Ayers Rock, an enormous sandstone rock rising about 1,100 feet above the surrounding land.

⊙ **In-Flight Movie**

Take flight over Australia and the Pacific and explore the region from the air.

GUIDE ON THE SIDE

Regional Flyover

Analyze Visuals Read Regional Flyover and ask the following questions about the labeled satellite photo.

- How do you think the varied geography of New Zealand both helps and hurts its economy? (Sample: Tourists probably love visiting features like glaciers and mountains, yet both those landforms are difficult to farm.)

- How might life in the Pacific islands have changed in the past 75 years? (Sample: With improvements in transportation technology, Pacific islanders have probably been better able to communicate and do business with other places, as well as attract larger numbers of tourists.)

⊙ **Inflight Movie**

Before playing the Inflight Movie, ask
- What about Australia and other islands in the Pacific would be easier to see flying overhead than standing on the ground?
- How might looking down at the Pacific Ocean help you determine the height of islands?

ECONOMY

The Importance of Coconut Many Pacific Island economies depend heavily on their exports of coconut products, especially copra—dried coconut meat—and coconut oil, which is extracted from copra. Coconut oil is used in goods ranging from detergents to vegetable shortening. In the island nation of Kiribati, copra makes up 62 percent of all exports. Other nations, including Papua New Guinea and the Marshall Islands, have economies that rely heavily on other coconut products, including copra cake and coconut oil.

GUIDE ON THE SIDE

People, Land, and Resources

Analyze Visuals Draw students' attention to the population density map and its accompanying key.

- How would you describe population density in Australia and New Zealand? (Population density in Australia is highest along the eastern coast. In New Zealand, population density is highest along the eastern coast of South Island and throughout much of North Island.)

- Where is population density lowest in Australia and New Zealand? What do these areas have in common? (Population density is lowest on the western half of each island and in the interior. These regions are drier and often mountainous.)

- What geographic factors might explain why population density varies so much in the Pacific? (Sample: Some factors might be distance from other islands, the low altitude of some islands, a challenging climate, and the distribution of natural resources.)

Regional Overview
Human Geography

People, Land, and Resources

The Pacific region's physical features have shaped where people in the region live. Most Australians and New Zealanders live in dense urban areas near the ocean. Few people live in Australia's dry deserts or in New Zealand's rugged mountains. The population of the smaller Pacific islands is generally more rural. Most people live in small villages.

Some countries in the region have many natural resources. Others are less fortunate. Australia and New Zealand's many resources have led to strong industrial economies. However, the economies of the smaller islands are generally limited by a lack of resources. Most smaller islands have developing economies, and many islanders fish or farm.

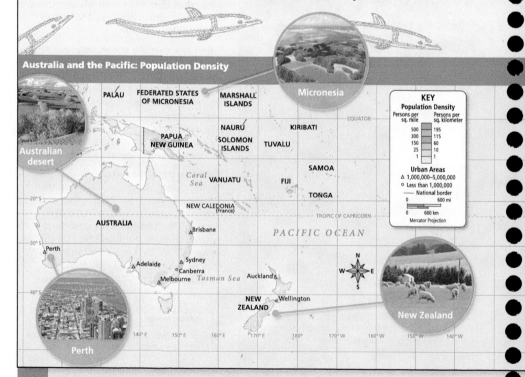

Australia and the Pacific: Population Density

CORE CONCEPTS: POPULATION DISTRIBUTION

Review Core Concepts 6.2 to help students understand how population density numbers can be confusing if one does not understand how they are calculated. For example, although the Federated States of Micronesia has a higher population density than some of the other nations shown in the graphic, its people are spread out across four major island groups that consist of 607 islands.

Half the population lives in one of these island groups, the Chuuk state, while another third lives in the Pohnpei state. The other two groups, Yap and Kosrae, each have about ten percent of the nation's population. On the nation's high islands, people settle near the coast; on its low atolls, people are usually only found in the interior, facing the lagoon.

my World IN NUMBERS

	Australia	Federated States of Micronesia	New Zealand	Palau	Tonga	Tuvalu	United States
Population	21 million	108,000	4.2 million	21,000	119,000	9,600	304 million
Population density (people per square mile)	7	397	40	119	430	1,218	86
GDP per capita	$37,300	$2,300	$27,200	$7,600	$5,100	$1,552	$45,800

SOURCE: *CIA World Factbook, Encyclopaedia Britannica*

Put It Together

1. What might be the advantages and disadvantages of living on a small Pacific island?

2. Remember that GDP per capita is the total economic output per person in a country. What geographic factors might influence the numbers for this region?

3. What seems to be the relationship between land and population? Between land and economy?

Data Discovery

Find your own data to make a regional data table.

Size Comparison

Australia is slightly smaller than the 48 contiguous states of the United States.

myWorld in Numbers

Analyze Visuals Point out the diagram and use the questions below to help students analyze the data and draw conclusions.

- Compare the GDP per capita of the United States with that of the other nations listed in the diagram. (It is much larger than GDP per capita in most of the other countries.)

- Why does it make sense that population density in Tuvalu is higher than in New Zealand? (Tuvalu has much less land area than New Zealand.)

- What other information would be helpful to better understand the region's population and economy? (Sample: land area, major industries, population distribution)

Data Discovery

Students can practice chart and graph skills online with the Data Discovery features on Australia and the Pacific. They can use their trackers to save data for their On Assignment story later in the unit.

PUT IT TOGETHER 1. Sample: Advantages: know your neighbors, few crowds or traffic jams; Disadvantages: less land for farming, fewer cultural and economic opportunities. **2. Sample:** amount of land, length of coasts.

3. Sample: It appears that the smaller the amount of land is, the higher population density will be. It also appears that countries with more land have more successful economies.

Plan With Understanding by Design*

Chapter Objectives
Begin With the End in Mind

Students will demonstrate the following enduring understandings:
- Colonization can have far-reaching and negative effects on a region's people, culture, and resources.
- Climate and location relative to resources influence where people migrate to and settle.
- A nation's development is closely linked to the region's past economic and cultural relationships.

Connect
Make Learning Meaningful

Student Edition
- **Essential Question** What makes a nation?
- **myStory** Jack keeps his family's Maori heritage alive while in school.

my worldgeography.com
myStory Video Get to know Jack through a video of his life and home.

Student Journal
Essential Question Preview

Experience
Teach Knowledge and Skills

Student Edition
- Read Sections 1, 2, 3, and 4.
- Answer Reading Checks and Section Assessment questions.

my worldgeography.com
On Assignment Visual Glossary, Active Atlas, Data Discovery, Language Lesson, Culture Close-up

Student Journal
- Sections 1, 2, 3, and 4 Word Wise
- Sections 1, 2, 3, and 4 Take Notes

Teacher's Edition
myWorld Activities
- Section 1: Travel Tips, p. T10
- Section 2: Before and After, p. T16
- Section 3: Take Action on the Pacific Environment, p. T24
- Section 4: Dear Antarctica, p. T32

21st Century Learning Online Tutor
- Read Physical Maps
- Identify Evidence
- Sequence
- Develop Cultural Awareness
- Identify Main Ideas and Details
- Generate New Ideas
- Summarize
- Ask Questions

Understand
Assess Understanding

Assessment Booklet
- Chapter Tests   • Benchmark Tests

Teacher's Edition
myWorld Chapter Activity
Students act as James Cook's crew to prepare a presentation on the region for the king of Great Britain.

Student Journal
Essential Question Writer's Workshop

my worldgeography.com
On Assignment Students will take a digital trip to Australia and the Pacific to examine what makes a nation.

Success ☆ Tracker™
Online at myworldgeography.com
Administer chapter tests and remediate understanding.

Student Edition
Chapter Assessment

"Understanding by Design" is registered as a trademark with the Patent and Trademark Office by the Association for Supervision of Curriculum Development (ASCD). ASCD has not authorized, approved or sponsored this work and is in no way affiliated with Pearson or its products.

Connect to the Essential Question

 Essential Question

What makes a nation?

Use the Essential Question poster and follow these steps to help students understand the Essential Question.

Connect to Their Lives

1. Ask students to think about foreign nations that they have visited, read about, or seen in TV shows and movies. What makes those nations different from the United States? As students share their answers with the class, list them on the board.

2. Then ask students to sort the different answers by the following categories: institutions, geography, culture, other. Post the following table for them to complete or have students turn to the *Essential Question Preview* page in their **Student Journal.**

Things That Make Nations Different from Each Other			
Institutions	**Geography**	**Culture**	**Other**

Connect to the Content

3. Now ask students to suppose that they are going to found a new nation. Ask, *What are the most important, most essential things that your nation would need?*

4. Post the following concept web on the board. Have students use it to record their ideas about what makes a nation.

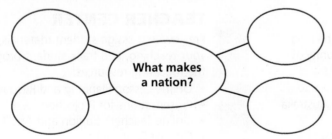

5. After previewing the chapter, have students make chapter-related predictions on the *Essential Question Preview* page in the **Student Journal.**

6. Remind students that they will answer a prompt related to the Essential Question on each section's *Take Notes* page in the **Student Journal.**

Explore  worldgeography.com

Welcome to myWorldGeography

http://www.myworldgeography.com

ON ASSIGNMENT: Australia and the Pacific

For this chapter's assignment, students will

- Take a digital trip to Australia and the Pacific.
- Take on the role of a journalist.
- Gather notes, images, and data throughout their journey.
- Write an article or create a multimedia slideshow connecting the information and images gathered during their trip and this chapter's Essential Question: *What makes a nation?*

ITINERARY

During their trip, students will make the following stops:

 myStory Video

Learn more about how Jack identifies with his Maori heritage.

 Active Atlas

Read more maps of Australia and the Pacific.

 Data Discovery

Gather data from more tables about life and economy in the region.

 Language Lesson

Learn how to greet people in the native Maori language, Te Reo Maori.

 Culture Close-up

Explore the mining town of Coober Pedy, South Australia.

 Self-Test

Assess their own knowledge of chapter content.

While on their trip, students will practice the following skills:

- **Investigate** the role of physical geography on regional settlement and development.
- **Identify** common characteristics of nations.

TIGed
TakingITGlobal for Educators

Extend the reach of every lesson by helping students connect to a global community of young people with common interests and concerns. Visit myworldgeography.com to

- explore Country Pages relating to Australia and the Pacific.
- delve deeper into this chapter's Essential Question, *What makes a nation?*
- find online alternatives to and solutions for the Unit Closer 21st Century Learning Activity.

my worldgeography.com

TEACHER CENTER

Preview and assign student materials, enrich your teaching, and track student progress with the following resources:

- Online Lesson Planning and Resource Library
- Presentations for Projection
- Online Teacher's Edition and Ancillaries
- Google Earth Links

Assess Enduring Understandings

myWorld Chapter Activity | **Step-by-Step Instructions** 🕐 2 hr 👥

Reporting Back: A Voyage to the Pacific

Teach this activity at the end of the chapter to assess enduring understandings.

OBJECTIVES

Students will demonstrate the following enduring understandings:

- Colonization can have far-reaching and negative effects on a region's people, culture, and resources.
- Climate and location relative to resources influence where people migrate to and settle.

Students will provide the following evidence of understanding:

- Expedition notes
- Multimedia presentation to the king

LEARNING STYLES

- Verbal
- Visual

MATERIALS

- Activity Support: Student Instructions and Rubric, p. T6
- Activity Support: Presentation Plan, p. T7
- Computers with slideshow software or posterboard
- Activity Cards: #139–144

  139. Voyage of the *Endeavour*, 1768–1771
  140. Lieutenant Cook's Journal
  141. People
  142. Plants and Animals
  143. Climate
  144. Resources

Activity Steps

1. **Describe the Project** Explain to students that they will represent crew members on James Cook's first voyage to Australia and New Zealand. Working in groups, students will use information from the Activity Cards, the chapter, and myworldgeography.com to make a slideshow, poster, or scroll presentation to the king of Great Britain, convincing him to support more expeditions or colonies in the region. Review *Activity Support: Student Instructions and Rubric* on the following page.

2. **Assign Roles** Divide students into six small groups. (If your class does not divide equally by six, combine roles.) Assign each student a role and provide a copy of the corresponding card: 139: Officer, 140: Captain's Scribe, 141: Anthropologist, 142: Biologist, 143: Climatologist, and 144: Economist. Students should take notes about their cards and related chapter information in order to brief their crew on their area of expertise.

3. **Crew Meeting** Have students report back to their crews with the information they have collected. Each student should take notes on every topic. Remind students that they are presenting to a king who

knows little about the region. Encourage students to think about what the king would most need to know, especially in relation to the area's potential as a colony.

L2 Extra Support If students feel overwhelmed by information, help them make a chart that separates information about Australia from information about New Zealand.

4. **Presentation to the King** Tell students to combine their findings to create a comprehensive, persuasive, and well-organized slideshow, poster presentation, or scroll presentation. Ask them to make the presentation as multifaceted as possible, such as with animation, audio, illustrations, collages, and text. (A digital presentation is historically inaccurate, but allowing alternative media may motivate some students.)

ELL Intermediate Give students a list of terms and phrases that will help them describe advantages and disadvantages of the region, such as *benefit, potential, promising, poor, not recommended,* and so on.

Name _____ Class _____ Date _____

myWorld Chapter Activity Support   **Student Instructions and Rubric**

Reporting Back: A Voyage to the Pacific

Activity Instructions Read the following summary of your myWorld Chapter Activity. Follow your teacher's directions for more information.

1. Work with your fellow "crew" members to gather information about Captain Cook's journey to the region. Take careful notes *on Activity Support: Presentation Plan.*

2. As a group, use your notes to plan a presentation to the king of Great Britain. Select the best maps, graphics, text, and/or audio and animation from each member's research. Your presentation should describe Australia and New Zealand, including their accessibility, distance from Great Britain, native peoples, indigenous plants and animals, climate, economic resources, and geographic features. Be sure to address the following questions:
   a. How can Great Britain benefit from the natural resources and location of Australia and New Zealand?
   b. What parts of the region would be easiest and most rewarding to settle? Explain.
   c. Why would it be worthwhile for British settlers to travel to this region despite its distance?

3. Practice key points of your presentation. Then present to the "king," your teacher.

myWorld Chapter Activity Rubric	3 Exceeds Understanding	2 Reaches Understanding	1 Approaches Understanding
Group Participation	Participates fully in gathering the data for the topic assigned; analyzes data to reach creative, accurate conclusions	Helps gather data; analyzes data to reach expected conclusions	Able to describe the data collected; performs little analysis of data
Presentation Planning	Listens to input of others; contributes to the group plan through research, detailed written work, and development of graphics	Contributes to planning the report by sharing clear ideas from research	Understands the plan for the group report; shares vague information from research
Presentation Creation	Highly engaged in the team presentation; helps to create detailed and accurate maps and graphics; no spelling or grammar errors in report	Mostly engaged in team presentation; assists with maps and graphics; few spelling or grammar errors	Helps some with the presentation of the report; plays small role in developing maps and graphics; some spelling and grammar errors inhibit understanding

Name _____ Class _____ Date _____

myWorld Chapter Activity Support Presentation Plan

Reporting Back: A Voyage to the Pacific

Directions Use this Activity Support to record your notes about the Activity Card assigned to you. Consider how you will explain your information to your expedition team. Then take notes on the information your fellow crew members share with you.

Important Information about Australia and New Zealand for the King	Notes	Key Points for the Presentation
General Information (location, dates, and so on)		
Cook's Journal		
People		
Plants and Animals		
Climate		
Resources		

Australia and the Pacific

- Introduce the Essential Question so that students will be able to understand the big ideas of this chapter (see earlier page, Connect to the Essential Question).

- Help students prepare to learn about Australia and the Pacific by looking at the chapter's maps, charts, and photos.

- Have students make and record chapter predictions with the *Essential Question Preview* in the **Student Journal.**

- Ask students to analyze maps on this page.

GUIDE ON THE SIDE

Explore the Essential Question . . .

Have students complete the Essential Question Writer's Workshop in their **Student Journal** to demonstrate in-depth understanding of the question in the context of this chapter.

Analyze Maps Have students examine first the political map and then the inset map.

- How does New Zealand's location compare to that of the United States? (New Zealand is located in the Southern and Eastern Hemispheres. The United States is in the Northern and Western Hemispheres.)

- How would you describe Australia and New Zealand in relation to the rest of the world? (Sample: isolated)

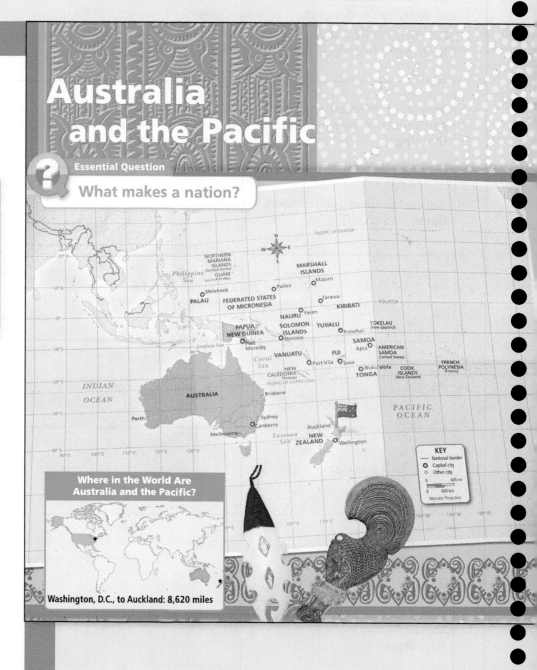

Australia and the Pacific

Essential Question

What makes a nation?

Where in the World Are Australia and the Pacific?

Washington, D.C., to Auckland: 8,620 miles

INTRODUCE my Story

Get Students excited to learn about Australia and the Pacific by first experiencing the region through the eyes of Jack, a young Maori New Zealander.

• Read myStory and watch the myStory Video about Jack's life.

• Have students complete *Jack Connects to His Culture* in the **Student Journal** to review what they learned about the Maori culture in New Zealand.

my Story

Jack Connects to His Culture

In this section, you'll read about Jack, a young man from New Zealand trying to keep in touch with his Maori culture. *What does Jack's story tell you about life in Australia and the Pacific?*

Story by Tui Ruwhiu for myWorld Geography Online

It is early one weekday morning, and 17-year-old Jack is busy getting ready for another day at school. Jack lives in Auckland, New Zealand's largest city. By 7:30, Jack is on the bus for the 50-minute ride to his school, Avondale College.

Jack lives with his two younger brothers and his mother, father, and grandmother. Jack's father is a television actor and comedian. His mother manages the household and works in a television production company.

Jack is part Maori (MAow ree), descended from the original inhabitants of New Zealand. The Maori migrated to New Zealand—which they call Aotearoa (AOW tee AR roh uh)—from other parts of the Pacific region about 1,000 years ago.

Explore the Essential Question
• at my worldgeography.com
• using the myWorld Chapter Activity
• with the Student Journal

Facial expressions like Jack's were often used by Maori to frighten enemies before battle. Today, Maori people make this expression as part of a traditional greeting on important occasions. ▶

my Story

Jack Connects to His Culture

• **Summarize** Who is Jack? Where does he live, and with whom? (Jack is part Maori, a seventeen-year-old student, and lives in Auckland with his brothers, parents, and grandmother.)

• **Connect** Did the Maori always live in New Zealand? (No. The Maori migrated to New Zealand from other parts of the Pacific region.)

NOTES

QUICK FACTS

The Maori At the beginning of the 2000s, there were more than 500,000 Maori in New Zealand, constituting about 15 percent of the country's population. Demographers estimate that this number will jump to 750,000, or 16.6 percent, by 2021. The majority of Maori live in New Zealand's cities, with only 16 percent living in rural and tribal areas. The years following World War II saw a mass migration of Maori to cities in search of better employment opportunities.

GUIDE ON THE SIDE

- **Identify Main Ideas** How are Maori citizens reclaiming their cultural identity? (They are trying to learn more about their native language, history, and culture.)

- **Infer** What do the wharenui and wharekai at Jack's school tell you about Maori culture in New Zealand schools? (Sample: New Zealand schools wish to honor and preserve the culture of the country's original inhabitants.)

- **Draw Conclusions** What does the loss of Maori culture and language tell you about New Zealand's European settlers? (Their presence, language, and traditions have largely replaced native Maori culture.)

Jack and his brothers

Jack and his horse

Maori students make up about 8 percent of the 2,600 students at Avondale College. They have their own wharenui (meeting house) and wharekai (dining hall) at school. At breaks, lunchtimes, and after school, Maori students gather at the wharekai to talk and share food with friends.

But Maori people like Jack and his friends once faced many obstacles in New Zealand. During the 1800s, British colonization of New Zealand led to a series of wars with the Maori. Eventually, the British defeated the Maori. Many Maori moved to cities and lost touch with their culture.

Interest in Maori culture has grown since the mid-1900s. Today, many Maori study their language, history, and customs. Jack feels a strong connection to his culture and to his homeland on New Zealand's North Island. "I know the blood of my ancestors is in that soil," he says quietly, "because they gave their lives fighting for that land."

Jack takes a Maori language class at school every day. He hopes to become a skilled Maori speaker like his father, who grew up speaking Maori.

CULTURE

Te Reo Maori During the early years of the European settlement of New Zealand, Europeans and Maori communicated mainly by using the Te Reo Maori language. But its usage by colonists soon declined. By the 1900s, Te Reo Maori was spoken almost exclusively by Maori. Speaking the language was forbidden in schools, and Maori use also decreased. By the 1980s, less than 20 percent of Maori people were fluent in it.

Maori civil-rights protests and a renewed interest in Maori culture during the 1970s and 1980s led to a greater interest in Te Reo Maori. New Zealand's first bilingual school opened in 1978, and the first Maori-language radio station began broadcasting in 1983. Today, the Maori language is spoken at several levels in schools. There are 20 Maori-language radio stations and a Maori-language television station.

Jack's class practices kapa haka.

Jack's waka ama team

Although Jack went to a Maori-language day care center as a child, his parents decided to send him to English-language schools. English is the language most commonly spoken in New Zealand. At home, the family speaks English.

Jack stays connected to Maori culture in other ways. He is one of the leaders of his school's kapa haka team. Kapa haka is a performance art that combines singing and dancing. It uses parts of traditional Maori songs, dances, and combat techniques.

Each year, New Zealand holds a national competition for high school students of kapa haka. This competition is part of Polyfest, a celebration of Polynesian culture and dance. To prepare for the competition, Jack's kapa haka team practices each day at lunchtime and after school. It also practices for at least one full day each weekend.

Jack is also a member of his school's waka ama team. Waka ama are Maori canoes designed for use on the open ocean. Avondale has male, female, and mixed waka ama teams. Students of all ethnic backgrounds take part in the sport.

Jack plans to continue studying the Maori language and participating in kapa haka after he finishes school. He hopes to increase his understanding of his culture. "If you're interested, it's a lot easier to learn," Jack says. "There are a lot of people out there who have the knowledge. You've just got to be willing to go out and grab it."

▶ **myStory Video**
Join Jack as he shows you more about his life in New Zealand.

Meet the Journalist
Name Tui Ruwhiu
Favorite Moment Watching Jack's kapa haka team practice

GUIDE ON THE SIDE

- **Summarize** What is Jack's philosophy on learning new things? (There is always new knowledge to gain if you look in the right places.)

- **Identify Evidence** What does the membership of Jack's waka ama team say about New Zealanders' attitude toward different cultures? (People from different backgrounds can easily take part in activities that were not originally part of their culture.)

▶ **myStory Video**

Have students watch the video at myworldgeography.com about Jack's interest in his Maori culture. Tell students to use their trackers to collect images and data about life in New Zealand.

Chapter Atlas

OBJECTIVES

Students will know

- the diversity of physical features, climates, and natural resources in the Pacific region.
- how and why people have chosen to settle in different areas of the region.

Students will be able to

- use maps to identify distances and differences in physical geography.
- identify evidence that supports specific statements about the region's geography.

SET EXPECTATIONS

In this section, students will

- read Chapter Atlas.
- use section content to prepare for a trip to the region.
- go On Assignment in Australia and the Pacific.

CORE CONCEPTS

You may wish to teach or reteach the following lessons from the Core Concepts Handbook:

- Understanding Maps, p. 10
- Land Use, p. 50
- What is Culture?, p. 86

KEY

Differentiated Instruction	English Language Instruction		
L1 Special Needs **L2** Extra Support	**ELL** Beginner	**ELL** Early Intermediate	**ELL** Intermediate
L3 On-Level **L4** Challenge	**ELL** Early Advanced	**ELL** Advanced	

1 Connect
Make learning meaningful

Make Connections Remind students of the physical geography they observed in the myStory video about Jack. Ask them to identify features of New Zealand's environment that seem similar and different than features of their own.

ELL Beginner Help students begin to make comparisons in English by teaching them how to use *this, that, these,* and *those.*

Activate Prior Knowledge Prompt students to think about what they have learned about population distribution and settlement patterns in other regions of the world. Show them a physical map of Australia and ask them to predict patterns of population distribution. Prompt them to recall the types of locations that attract large numbers of people.

L2 Extra Support Remind students that human needs dictate where people settle. Post the categories *Food, Trade,* and *Natural Resources* and have students pick one place on the map that may relate to each and explain why.

Prepare Follow the steps in the section **Preview.** Preteach the Key Terms. Then have students complete *Word Wise* in their **Student Journal** using in-text clues and the glossary for help.

2 Experience
Teach knowledge and skills

Read Use **Background** notes and **Guide on the Side** questions to model active reading. Have students use *Take Notes* in their **Student Journal** to record important places to know in Australia and the Pacific on an outline map. Students should use the maps in the Chapter Atlas and the Active Atlas at myworldgeography.com for assistance.

ELL Early Intermediate Review cardinal directions (north, south, east, west) and terms such as *right, left,* and *straight.* Have partners use section maps and text to give each other directions between two points in Australia.

L3 On-Level Have students read and complete *Enrichment: Kiwi: More Than Just a Bird.*

Practice: myWorld Activity Students will use information about physical geography, climate, population distribution, and natural resources to advise travelers on how to prepare for a visit to the region. **Step-by-Step Instructions** and **More Activities** follow on pp. T10–T11.

SECTION 1 RESOURCE GUIDE

FOR THE STUDENT

my worldgeography.com Student Center

- Visual Glossary
- Active Atlas

Student Edition (print and online)

- Geographic Atlas

Student Journal (print and online)

- Section 1 Word Wise
- Section 1 Take Notes

21st Century Learning Online Tutor

- Read Physical Maps
- Identify Evidence

FOR THE TEACHER

my worldgeography.com Teacher Center

- Online Lesson Planner
- Presentations for Projection
- SuccessTracker

ProGuide: Australia and the Pacific

- Lesson Plan, pp. T8–T9
- myWorld Activity Step-by-Step Instructions, p. T10
- Activity Support: Packing Plan, p. T11
- myWorld Geography Enrichment, p. T12
- Section Quiz, p. T13

Accelerating the Progress of ELLs

- Peer Learning Strategies, p. 46

3 Understand
Assess understanding

Review Review *Word Wise* and *Take Notes* in the **Student Journal.**

Assess Knowledge and Skills Use the Section Assessment and Section Quiz to check students' progress.

Assess Understanding Review students' responses to the Section Assessment Essential Question prompt.

Remediate Use these strategies to review and remediate.

If students struggle to . . .	Try these strategies.
Differentiate Australia and New Zealand from the Pacific Islands	Have students color-code the maps in the **Student Journal** and make corresponding concept webs.
Identify settlement patterns in the region	Have students review migration chronology using the **Online Student Edition.**
Understand the difficulties of some low-lying islands	Show aerial photographs and have students compare risks of living on a beach or a mountain.

ELL Support

ELL Objective Students will be able to categorize English geography terms.

Cultural Connections Have students describe in their home languages the most heavily populated areas of their current communities or familiar countries. Ask them to share their opinions on why these places attract so many people.

ELL Early Advanced Content Tip Have students create a word bank about Australia or New Zealand and then sort their suggestions into categories like *Climate* and *Natural Resources.* Challenge students to briefly state how each word connects to its category.

 ELL Activity Review opposites. Then give partners a photocopied map of the Pacific region and a list of labels like *dry, warm, high, low, large population,* and *small population.* Direct students to label the map with the comparative terms, drawing a line between the places being compared. Tell them to try to use each label at least twice. **(Visual)**

myWorld Activity   **Step-by-Step Instructions**

 30 min

Travel Tips

OBJECTIVES

Students will

- draw conclusions about the effects of climate, geography, and population.
- identify evidence for why tourism develops.

LEARNING STYLE

- Verbal
- Visual

21st Century Learning

- Identify Evidence

MATERIALS

- Posterboard or chart paper
- Tape
- Activity Support: Packing Plan, p. T11

Activity Steps

1. Tell students that they are going to write a brief travel guide for the Pacific region. They will then use what they write to suggest two different things to pack for a trip to the region.

2. Give students a copy of *Activity Support: Packing Plan*. Ask them to use what they learned in Section 1 to fill out the categories on the handout. Remind them to think about how different elements of geography might affect tourism, such as sightseeing where interesting landforms exist.

   L1 Special Needs Have students describe what they packed the last time they used a bag or suitcase. Ask why they packed each item, helping students see how climate, geography, and plans affected their choices.

3. Tell students to illustrate two items from their list that people planning to visit the Pacific region should pack. They should cut out these illustrations and

prepare to explain their choices. Encourage creativity. For example, they may want to pack an appetite for the region's bananas and cocoa, or bottled water for visits to the sometimes-dry atoll islands.

4. Using chart paper or posterboard, draw three "suitcases," one for Australia, one for New Zealand, and one for the Pacific islands, and post them at the front of the room. Ask students to come "pack" the suitcases by taping their illustrations to the appropriate paper. They should explain in no more than two sentences why they think each item is a must-have for travel to the region.

   ELL Intermediate/Early Advanced Give students alternative ways of saying *because* in their explanations. Help them practice other subordinating conjunctions, such as *since*, *while*, and *in order to*.

More Activities From myWorld Teachers

 Local Connections Have students research and discuss where the water they drink, cook with, and bathe in comes from. Have students make annotated maps showing how water sources influence where people settle in the region. **(Verbal/Visual)**

Plate Plays Ask small groups to use the information in the section to role-play Australia and the Pacific region's history of plate tectonics. Tell them to model

what might have happened if the plates described in the text had moved in different directions. **(Kinesthetic)**

Map It! Have students use Google Earth to create a map tour of Australia and the Pacific. Tell them to mark or "pinpoint" well-known locations, such as Uluru, New Zealand's two major islands, or atoll nations. **(Visual)**

 my worldgeography.com (**Teacher Center** →) Find additional resources in the online Teacher Center.

Name _____ Class _____ Date _____

 myWorld Activity Support   **Packing Plan**

Travel Tips

Directions Imagine that you are a writer for the *Read Before You Go to . . . !* travel guide for Australia, New Zealand, and the Pacific islands. Write detailed travel tips that will help the traveler have a pleasant, exciting trip.

Read Before You Go to . . . Australia and the Pacific!

What kind of climate to expect: _____

_____

_____

What you can see and do: _____

_____

_____

_____

_____

_____

How to avoid crowds: _____

_____

_____

Now draw two items that travelers to the region might need.

Name _____ Class _____ Date _____

Enrichment: Kiwi: More Than Just a Bird

Directions Read the selection below. Answer the questions that follow and complete the activity.

For almost a hundred years, New Zealanders have had an unusual nickname: *kiwi*. The kiwi is a bird native to New Zealand, famous for not being able to fly. It has long whiskers and uses its nostrils to sniff out food. Since kiwis cannot fly, the birds are only found on the islands of New Zealand.

Although New Zealanders sometimes used the kiwi as a symbol of their country, it was not until World War I that *kiwi* became a nickname for the New Zealand people. Soldiers from other countries first used the nickname for New Zealanders, probably because they saw the bird on New Zealand military badges. New Zealand's troops also used a type of boot polish called Kiwi. In the years following World War I, New Zealanders began using the term *kiwi* to describe themselves. The name started to crop up all over the country. Soon everything, from the national lottery to a new form of currency, used the word *kiwi*.

Today, *kiwi* is widely accepted as a nickname in New Zealand. Sadly, the bird behind the nickname has not been helped by this popularity. All species of kiwi are now at risk of extinction. Predators, human activity, and loss of habitat have all harmed the national bird. Public and private programs are now trying to protect the kiwi population from further harm.

1. Why do you think the people of New Zealand began using *kiwi* as a nickname?

_____

_____

2. Reread the third paragraph of the selection above. What do you think the government should do to protect the kiwi?

_____

_____

3. Activity Research in more detail why kiwi are endangered. Create a "You Need to Know!" brochure that the New Zealand government might give to New Zealanders to help them better protect the kiwi.

Name _____ Class _____ Date _____

Section Quiz

Directions Answer the following questions using what you learned in Section 1.

1. _____ The Pacific islands formed by coral reefs are called
   a. volcanic.
   b. reefs.
   c. atolls.
   d. plates.

2. _____ What was one effect of plate movement on the Pacific region?
   a. Australia and New Zealand became connected to North America.
   b. Plate movement isolated many species.
   c. Few volcanoes formed.
   d. The regional climate grew much colder.

3. _____ Where in Australia can you find a dry climate, few people, and low plateaus and plains?
   a. Great Barrier Reef
   b. Outback
   c. high islands
   d. the eastern coast

4. _____ A coral reef is a rock-like collection of
   a. dried volcanic lava.
   b. tiny skeletons.
   c. sand.
   d. sea salt.

5. _____ How does the availability of natural resources vary among Australia, New Zealand, and the Pacific islands?
   a. All the islands struggle to find enough water.
   b. The same natural resources are found across the region.
   c. Lower islands tend to have more water.
   d. More natural resources are found on higher islands.

6. Compare and contrast the climate, physical geography, population, and natural resources of Australia and Polynesia using the table below.

	Just Australia	**Both Australia and Polynesia**	**Just Polynesia**
Climate			
Physical Geography			
Population			
Natural Resources			

Chapter Atlas

- Model preparing to read by previewing the Key Ideas, Key Terms, headings, visuals, and captions. Have students make predictions about what they will learn. For ELL support, post the prompt "I predict I will read about . . ."

- Preview and practice the reading skill, Read Physical Maps, by asking students to look at the different geographic features on a physical map of your region, including landforms and distances.

- Preteach this section's high-use Academic Vocabulary and Key Terms using the chart on the next page and in-text definitions. Have students practice Key Terms by completing the *Word Wise* page in their **Student Journal.**

GUIDE ON THE SIDE

Physical Features

- **Read Maps** Where is Australia located? (Australia is located in the southwest Pacific Ocean, between Southeast Asia and Antarctica.)

- **Infer** Given their distance from other, heavily settled areas, how might some islands in the Pacific region have developed differently than much of the rest of the world? (Sample: Remote islands may have had less access to new technologies. Also, immigration may have been minimal, which would have helped islands maintain their cultural traditions for many years.)

Reading Skill

Label an Outline Map While they read, have students identify the Places to Know! on the outline map of the region in the **Student Journal.**

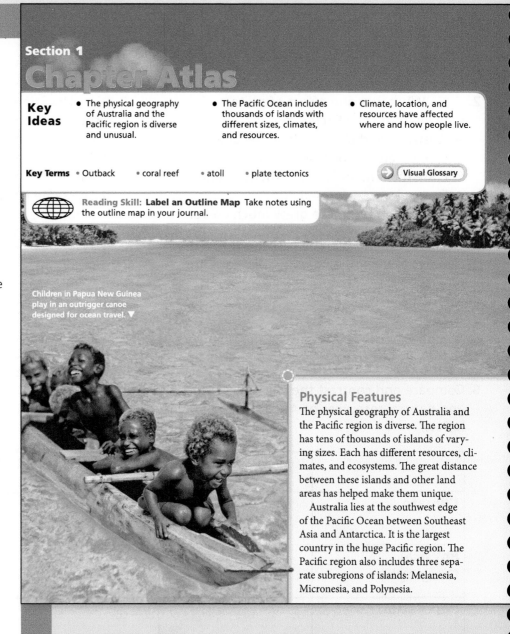

Section 1

Chapter Atlas

Key Ideas
- The physical geography of Australia and the Pacific region is diverse and unusual.
- The Pacific Ocean includes thousands of islands with different sizes, climates, and resources.
- Climate, location, and resources have affected where and how people live.

Key Terms • Outback • coral reef • atoll • plate tectonics

Visual Glossary

Reading Skill: Label an Outline Map Take notes using the outline map in your journal.

Children in Papua New Guinea play in an outrigger canoe designed for ocean travel. ▼

Physical Features

The physical geography of Australia and the Pacific region is diverse. The region has tens of thousands of islands of varying sizes. Each has different resources, climates, and ecosystems. The great distance between these islands and other land areas has helped make them unique.

Australia lies at the southwest edge of the Pacific Ocean between Southeast Asia and Antarctica. It is the largest country in the huge Pacific region. The Pacific region also includes three separate subregions of islands: Melanesia, Micronesia, and Polynesia.

ACADEMIC VOCABULARY

High-Use Word	Definition and Sample Sentence
distinct	*adj.* different *She decided to divide her essay into three distinct parts: an introduction, a body, and a conclusion.*
collide	*v.* to come together *The two cars collided when one driver failed to stop for a red light.*

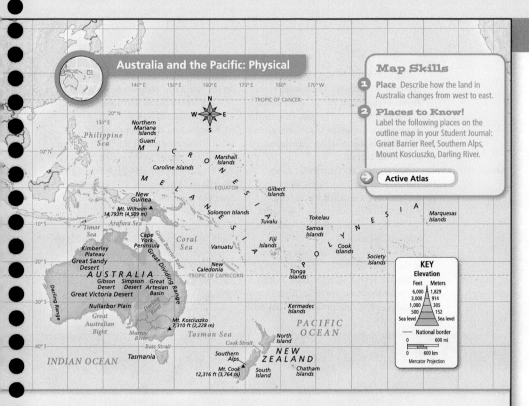

Australia and the Pacific: Physical

Map Skills

1. **Place** Describe how the land in Australia changes from west to east.

2. **Places to Know!** Label the following places on the outline map in your Student Journal: Great Barrier Reef, Southern Alps, Mount Kosciuszko, Darling River.

Active Atlas

KEY
Elevation

Feet	Meters
6,000	1,829
3,000	914
1,000	305
500	152
Sea level	Sea level

— National border

0   600 mi
0   600 km
Mercator Projection

GUIDE ON THE SIDE

Map Skills Have students examine the map to identify geographic characteristics of the Pacific region.

- **Read Physical Maps** Which northern Pacific island has large areas of high elevation? (New Guinea)

- **Infer** Why do you think more people live in eastern Australia than in the Outback? (Eastern Australia has more water and fertile land.)

- **Draw Conclusions** Australia is different in many ways from the other continents. Why do you think it is considered a continent? (Sample: Australia is too large to be called an island, plus it is far enough away from other continents to keep it from being considered part of them.)

Australia is completely surrounded by water, just like an island. But because of its large size, it is considered a continent. It is Earth's smallest continent.

Australia has wide, flat stretches of dry land, especially in its central and western portions. The interior of Australia is known as the **Outback,** a sparsely inhabited region with low plateaus and plains. The Outback is home to a large rock formation known as Uluru, or Ayers Rock. Central and western Australia include three large deserts—the Great Victoria Desert, the Great Sandy Desert, and the Simpson Desert. Eastern Australia, on the other hand, is covered by low mountains, valleys, and a large river system. Australia's coasts also include fertile plains.

Australia's dramatic physical features are not limited to land. The Great Barrier Reef, located off Australia's northeast coast, is the world's largest grouping of coral reefs. A **coral reef** is a formation of rock-like material made up of the skeletons of tiny sea creatures. The Great Barrier Reef is more than 1,250 miles (2,000 kilometers) long. It is home to many different underwater plants and animals. It is also a popular place for surfing and scuba diving.

Active Atlas

Have students go to myworldgeography.com to further examine maps of Australia and the Pacific.

MAP SKILLS 1. In Australia, elevation changes from high to low to high again, finally returning to low at the eastern coast. **2.** Students should use the section map to mark the appropriate locations in their **Student Journal.**

ANSWERS

HISTORY

Greek in the Pacific The names of the island groups that make up the Pacific islands reflect the European explorers who first came up with the titles. *Melanesia* comes from the Greek for "dark islands," a reference to inhabitants' skin color. *Micronesia* comes from the Greek for "small islands," a description that does fit the atolls and small coral islands that make up the majority of the region. *Polynesia* comes from the less specific Greek for "many islands."

- **Compare and Contrast** Are coral islands lower or higher than volcanic islands? (lower)
- **Predict** Do you think the size of islands affects their economic development? Explain. (Sample: Small islands probably have fewer natural resources. This may make improving the economy a difficult task.)

Analyze Visuals Ask students to describe in their own words how atolls are formed over time.

- What survives longer during a toll formation: the coral or the island? (the coral)

The subregion Melanesia lies just north and east of Australia. The islands in this group stretch from Papua New Guinea in the west to Fiji in the east. Despite the remote location of many of these islands, Melanesia is the most densely populated part of the region.

More than 2,000 small islands are located north of Melanesia. Together, these islands are called Micronesia. Almost all of the islands in this part of the Pacific are made of coral, and most have sandy beaches.

The third—and largest—subregion in the South Pacific is Polynesia. This subregion forms a rough triangle. It stretches thousands of miles from New Zealand in the southwest to the Hawaiian Islands in the north and to Easter Island in the southeast. New Zealand's mountainous North Island and South Island are the largest islands in Polynesia.

Polynesia includes thousands of small islands scattered across the Pacific Ocean. Like other islands in the region, they can be divided into two <u>distinct</u> types: high islands and low islands. High islands are mountainous, rocky, and volcanic. They have very fertile soil.

Low islands are located just above sea level. Most have poor, sandy soil and little fresh water. Many low islands are atolls. An **atoll** is a ring-shaped coral island enclosing a body of water.

distinct, *adj.,* different

Reading Check What are the three subregions of the Pacific region?

Atoll Formation

The diagram below shows how an atoll (right) is formed. **1** An atoll begins as a coral reef around a volcanic island. **2** The coral builds as the island wears away over time. **3** Finally, only a ring of coral remains.

READING CHECK Melanesia, Micronesia, Polynesia

QUICK FACTS

Mariana Trench The deepest part of Earth's ocean floors is found just east of the Mariana Islands and is known as the Mariana Trench. Arc-shaped with an average width of 40 miles, the trench is the result of subduction: one plate meeting another and riding over it. The trench's deepest point, named Challenger Deep after the vessel that discovered it in 1951, is 36,198 feet deep. This depth is more than 7,000 feet greater than the height of Mount Everest above sea level.

Plate Tectonics

Plate tectonics helps us understand the forces that have shaped Australia and the Pacific. **Plate tectonics** is the theory that explains how huge blocks of Earth's crust called "plates" move. Hundreds of millions of years ago, the region was part of a giant continent. This ancient continent also included the land that now makes up South America, Africa, and India. Over time, Earth's plates separated. The giant continent slowly broke apart.

Australia and the Pacific include the Indo-Australian and Pacific plates. These two plates move toward each other at a rate of a few inches per year. Although this movement is slow, it has important effects on the region. As the plates collide, they push the ocean floor up above sea level. This creates many islands and volcanoes along the plate boundaries.

Plate movement and volcanic action have formed the two main islands of New Zealand. North Island has a series of high volcanic peaks that tower over green valleys below. South Island's Southern Alps are even higher mountains running along the island's western edge.

The movement of tectonic plates also helps explain the region's unique plant and animal populations. After the region broke away from other areas millions of years ago, its plants and animals were cut off from the rest of the world.

collide, *v.*, to come together

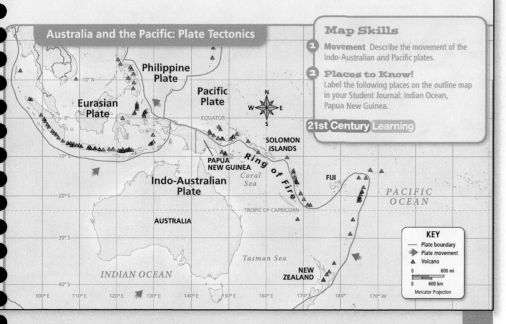

Australia and the Pacific: Plate Tectonics

Philippine Plate

Pacific Plate

Eurasian Plate

EQUATOR

SOLOMON ISLANDS

PAPUA NEW GUINEA

Indo-Australian Plate

Coral Sea

Ring of Fire

FIJI

PACIFIC OCEAN

TROPIC OF CAPRICORN

AUSTRALIA

Tasman Sea

INDIAN OCEAN

NEW ZEALAND

KEY
— Plate boundary
➤ Plate movement
▲ Volcano

0   600 mi
0   600 km
Mercator Projection

Map Skills

1 **Movement** Describe the movement of the Indo-Australian and Pacific plates.

2 **Places to Know!** Label the following places on the outline map in your Student Journal: Indian Ocean, Papua New Guinea.

21st Century Learning

MAP SKILLS 1. The two plates are slowly moving toward each other.
2. Students should use the section map to mark the appropriate locations in their **Student Journal.**

Map Skills Have students use the map to trace plate movement with their fingers.

- What do most of the plate boundaries have in common? (Most are lined with volcanoes.)

Plate Tectonics

- **Summarize** Hundreds of millions of years ago, what did South America and Australia have in common? (They were both part of the same giant continent.)

- **Predict** Do you think plate tectonics will continue to change the way the Pacific region looks? Explain. (Yes. Since the plates are still moving, they will produce new volcanoes and therefore new islands.)

21st Century Learning

Read Physical Maps Have students develop this skill by using this interactive online tutorial and activities. Students will learn to draw conclusions about regions from physical maps.

ANSWERS

QUICK FACTS

The Freo Doctor During what can be extremely hot summers, one source of relief for Australians living in the southwest is the wind known as the Fremantle, or Freo Doctor. These breezes blow across from the Indian Ocean on most summer afternoons, reaching 15 to 25 knots from October to March.

- **Summarize** How did nonnative plants and animals arrive in the Pacific region? (Many settlers brought species to the region.)

- **Connect** Why are Australia and the Pacific islands home to so many native species? (When continents broke apart, animals and plants on islands were isolated and did not move to other parts of the world.)

Climate

- **Summarize** What factors affect weather and climate in Australia and the Pacific Islands? (elevation, wind, ocean currents)

Over time, small changes have occurred naturally in the region's plants and animals. Because of the area's isolation, these changes have not spread to other places. As a result, Australia and the Pacific islands have many plant and animal species that cannot be found anywhere else in the world.

However, people have brought new plants and animals to the region. In some areas, the spread of nonnative species such as rabbits, snakes, and wild pigs has harmed the region's ecosystems.

Reading Check How has plate movement affected the region?

Climate

Weather and climate patterns vary widely across the Pacific region. Even opposite sides of the same island can have very different weather patterns due to differences in elevation, wind, and ocean currents.

Australia Australia's climate changes dramatically from one area to another. Its southeast and southwest coasts have temperate climates. The eastern coast has plentiful rainfall. In far northern Australia, heavy monsoon rains are common in the summer months. A winter dry season follows this wet season. However, most

Pacific Ecosystems

The Pacific region is so far from other places that many of its animals and plants are not found anywhere else on Earth. At right, a boab, a tree found only in Australia.

Koalas sleep for about 19 hours a day.

The platypus is a mammal that lays eggs.

A baby kangaroo lives in its mother's pouch.

READING CHECK Plate tectonics has created many volcanoes and islands and isolated many animal and plant species

GEOGRAPHY

New Zealand's Need for Rain Most of New Zealand averages between 23 and 63 inches of rain a year and has a mainly dry winter season. This rain is essential because 70 percent of the country's electricity is generated by hydroelectricity. Much of this power is drawn from major storage reservoirs, which can be either natural or artificial lakes. Three of these lakes provide about 70 percent of the water needed for hydroelectricity: Lake Pūkaki (in central South Island), Lake Tekapo (also in central South Island), and Lake Taupō (in central North Island).

of central Australia has arid and semiarid climates. This region has warm temperatures and little rain year-round.

New Zealand and the Pacific Islands New Zealand has a mild and wet maritime climate. It is cooler than Australia. Most other Pacific islands are located in the tropics. They tend to have tropical wet climates, with heavy precipitation and high temperatures year-round. On some mountainous islands, such as New Guinea, precipitation and temperature vary with elevation. Places at higher elevations usually have less rain and lower temperatures.

Water and Wildfires Although many of the Pacific islands receive heavy rainfall, some places still do not have enough fresh water for drinking or other human use. Low-lying atolls and low, sandy islands can collect very little rainwater.

Wildfires are a serious challenge in dry parts of the region. In Australia, fires can spread rapidly across the countryside during the winter dry season. These destructive fires are made worse by the grasses that grow during the summer wet weather and dry out during the winter.

Reading Check How do climates vary within Australia?

myWorld Activity
Traveling Tips

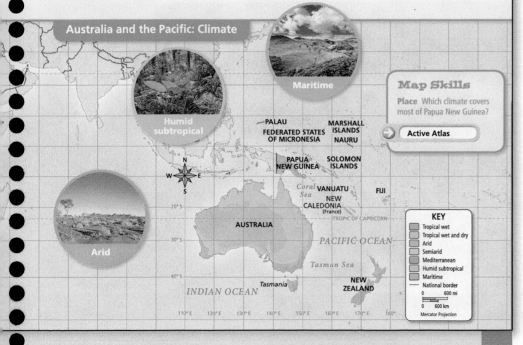

Australia and the Pacific: Climate

Maritime

Humid subtropical

Arid

PALAU
FEDERATED STATES OF MICRONESIA
MARSHALL ISLANDS
NAURU

PAPUA NEW GUINEA
SOLOMON ISLANDS

Coral Sea
VANUATU
NEW CALEDONIA (France)
FIJI

20° S

AUSTRALIA

30° S

PACIFIC OCEAN
TROPIC OF CAPRICORN

Map Skills
Place Which climate covers most of Papua New Guinea?

Active Atlas

KEY
Tropical wet
Tropical wet and dry
Arid
Semiarid
Mediterranean
Humid subtropical
Maritime
National border
0   600 mi
0 600 km
Mercator Projection

Tasman Sea

40° S

Tasmania
INDIAN OCEAN

NEW ZEALAND

110° E   120° E   130° E   140° E   150° E   160° E   170° E   180°

READING CHECK Much of Australia is semiarid or arid. Along the coasts, climates become moister, ranging from maritime and humid subtropical to Mediterranean and tropical wet and dry.

MAP SKILLS tropical wet

GUIDE ON THE SIDE

Map Skills Have students compare the climate differences shown on the map.

- Does New Zealand have a more or less consistent climate than Australia? Explain. (New Zealand has a more consistent climate. All of the country has a maritime climate, unlike Australia, which has six climate types.)

- **Analyze Cause and Effect** How do Australia's weather patterns help produce damaging wildfires? (Fire-prone grasses grow during the wet season and then dry out, helping fire to spread during the dry season.)

myWorld Activity

Traveling Tips Find Step-by-Step Instructions and an Activity Support on pp. T10–T11. **(Verbal/Visual)**

Active Atlas

Have students go to myworldgeography.com to further examine maps of Australia and the Pacific.

HISTORY

Australian Gold Rush Gold, one of Australia's important natural resources, had a major effect on the development of the country. In 1851, Australian Edward Hargraves, a veteran of the California Gold Rush, discovered gold near Bathurst. His discovery changed the future of the continent. Sizable amounts of gold were discovered in every part of the continent except South Australia.

People from all over the world poured into Australia, with 370,000 people arriving in 1852 alone. Although most new immigrants were from Europe and the United States, a large number were from China. These Chinese prospectors and laborers made up 3.3 percent of the Australian population by 1861, although most left after their work was done.

People and Resources

- **Compare and Contrast** Is population distribution similar in Australia and New Zealand? Explain. (Population patterns vary in Australia and New Zealand. Population density is heaviest in a few urban areas.)

Analyze Visuals Prompt students to analyze the photo and make connections between the various circle graphs.

- What does the photo tell you about the size of major cities in Australia as compared to the size of major cities in New Zealand? (Many of the areas of lights are brighter and bigger in Australia, meaning those cities probably have larger populations than any in New Zealand.)

- Are the odds of a person living in the city high or low in Melanesia? (low)

my **World**
IN NUMBERS

If there were
100 people
in the world,

51 would
live in cities.

People and Resources

The region's population patterns vary widely. The availability of natural resources also differs from place to place.

Australia and New Zealand Most Australians and New Zealanders live in urban areas. Most Australians live on the country's mild east coast. Nearly 90 percent of the country's 22 million people live in coastal cities such as Sydney and Melbourne. The hot, dry central area of Australia has fewer people.

Most of New Zealand's 4 million people live on North Island. This island includes Auckland and other cities.

Australia is rich in natural resources, including bauxite, iron, and diamonds. It also has energy resources such as coal and natural gas. New Zealand, however, has relatively few mineral resources.

Both Australia and New Zealand have many large farms and ranches. Australia produces cotton, wheat, and sheep, although lack of water is a big challenge

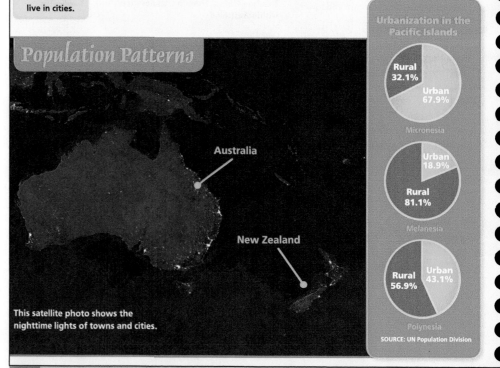

Population Patterns

Australia

New Zealand

This satellite photo shows the nighttime lights of towns and cities.

Urbanization in the Pacific Islands

Rural 32.1%
Urban 67.9%
Micronesia

Urban 18.9%
Rural 81.1%
Melanesia

Rural 56.9%
Urban 43.1%
Polynesia

SOURCE: UN Population Division

READING CHECK Population is much higher on islands with more plentiful resources, such as islands with higher elevations.

SECTION 1 ASSESSMENT **1.** Plate tectonics has created many volcanic islands and isolated species. **2.** The Outback is in the interior of Australia, with low population density, plains, and plateaus. **3.** A mostly dry climate and dry land have led people

ECONOMY

Tourism For many Pacific islands, some of the most important natural resources are the beauty of the land, a pleasingly tropical nightlife, and authentic cultural experiences. As transportation to remote locations has become easier, tourism to large and small Pacific islands has increased. In Fiji, approximately 550,000 tourists arrived in 2005—well more than half the island's native population of about 839,000. And in Palau, the native population of around 20,000 was far outnumbered by its 86,000 tourists in 2005.

for farmers and ranchers. Much of central Australia is too dry for agriculture or grazing. Irrigation is very important.

New Zealand's fertile farmland and supplies of fresh water support its successful agriculture. Wool production is important.

Pacific Islands The population of the Pacific islands is generally less urban than that of Australia and New Zealand. Many people live in small villages in hilly regions or on coastlines.

The availability of natural resources varies. Most of the low islands have poor soil, little vegetation, and few mineral or energy resources. As a result, the low islands have relatively small populations.

High islands have fertile soil and many natural resources. Their farms produce bananas, cacao, and other crops. Some high islands also have resources such as gold, copper, and petroleum.

Reading Check How does the availability of resources affect population in the region?

▲ Many Pacific economies rely on natural resources. Above, oil workers drill in Papua New Guinea.

Section 1 Assessment

Key Terms

1. How has the movement of tectonic plates affected the region?

2. Describe Australia's Outback region.

Key Ideas

3. How have Australia's geography and climate influenced where people live?

4. How do high islands differ from low islands?

5. How does the geography of the region vary from one place to another?

Think Critically

6. **Compare and Contrast** How do population and resources vary in different parts of the region?

7. **Draw Conclusions** Why are many Pacific species found nowhere else on Earth?

? Essential Question

What makes a nation?

8. How have climate, location, and resources affected the development of Australia, New Zealand, and the Pacific islands?

History of Australia and the Pacific

OBJECTIVES

Students will know

- how early people migrated to different parts of the Pacific.
- why colonization took place in the region and its effects on indigenous cultures.

Students will be able to

- sequence the chronology and effects of migration and settlement.
- address the cultural differences that resulted from colonization.

SET EXPECTATIONS

In this section, students will

- read History of Australia and the Pacific.
- identify changes related to colonization.
- go On Assignment in Australia and the Pacific.

CORE CONCEPTS

You may wish to teach or reteach the following lessons from the Core Concepts Handbook:

- Understanding Maps, p. 11
- Migration, p. 79
- Cultural Diffusion and Change, p. 97

KEY

Differentiated Instruction	English Language Instruction		
L1 Special Needs **L2** Extra Support	**ELL** Beginner	**ELL** Early Intermediate	**ELL** Intermediate
L3 On-Level **L4** Challenge	**ELL** Early Advanced	**ELL** Advanced	

1 Connect
Make learning meaningful

Make Connections Prompt students to think of what they packed the last time they stayed away from home, such as at a friend's house or summer camp. Ask them what they expected the place to have for them, like towels or toothpaste. Discuss why people moving to a new place might want it to resemble their old home. Ask them if there are particular mementos they might bring if they were going to stay for a long time in a new place.

L2 Extra Support Review the process and reasons behind migration explained in Core Concepts Lesson 6.3.

Activate Prior Knowledge Remind students that they learned about the climate and natural resources of Australia and the Pacific region in Section 1. Ask them to predict why these geographic factors might attract people to settle in the region.

ELL Advanced Introduce and explain the opposites pair *attractive* and *unappealing*. Ask students to find words or phrases in the previous section they think would fit into each category, such as *fertile* and *dry*.

Prepare Follow the steps in the section **Preview.** Preteach the Key Terms. Then have students complete *Word Wise* in their **Student Journal** using in-text clues and the glossary for help.

2 Experience
Teach knowledge and skills

Read Use **Background** notes and **Guide on the Side** questions to model active reading. Have students use *Take Notes* in their **Student Journal** to track the sequence of people's movements. Have students complete **21st Century Online Tutor** *Sequence,* and apply this skill to reading the section.

L4 Challenge Have students read *Enrichment: Cook and the Chronometer* and complete the accompanying activity.

ELL Intermediate Have student paraphrase one section of the text while a native English speaker records what he or she says. Allow the first student to then read over what he or she said and try to correct areas that seem unclear.

L1 Special Needs Have students read the **Online Student Edition** while listening to the accompanying audio.

Practice: myWorld Activity Students will identify the cultural and other changes that resulted from the European settlement of Australia and New Zealand. **Step-by-Step Instructions** and **More Activities** follow on pp. T16–T17.

SECTION 2 RESOURCE GUIDE

FOR THE STUDENT

my worldgeography.com Student Center

- Visual Glossary
- Active Atlas

Student Edition (print and online)

- History of Australia and the Pacific

Student Journal (print and online)

- Section 2 Word Wise
- Section 2 Take Notes

21st Century Learning Online Tutor

- Sequence
- Develop Cultural Awareness

FOR THE TEACHER

my worldgeography.com Teacher Center

- Online Lesson Planner
- Presentations for Projection
- SuccessTracker

ProGuide: Australia and the Pacific

- Lesson Plan, pp. T14–T15
- myWorld Activity Step-by-Step Instructions, p. T16
- Activity Support: Effective Illustrations, p. T17
- myWorld Geography Enrichment, p. T18
- Section Quiz, p. T19

Accelerating the Progress of ELLs

- Comprehension Check Strategies, p. 53

---

3 Understand
Assess understanding

Review Review Word Wise and Take Notes in the **Student Journal**.

Assess Knowledge and Skills Use the Section Assessment and Section Quiz to check students' progress.

Assess Understanding Review students' responses to the Section Assessment Essential Question prompt.

Remediate Use these strategies to review and remediate.

If students struggle to . . .	Try these strategies.
Understand Key Terms	Show relationships between terms using visual diagrams, such as *assimilation* and *missionary.*
Visualize the setting of information in section	Send students on an online treasure hunt to find images of specific places mentioned in the section.
Sequence the events and results of Pacific settlement	Help students create as-you-read timelines.

ELL Support

ELL Objective Students will be able to identify direct and indirect objects in English.

Cultural Connections Have students use both their home language and English to describe to a partner how their families and ancestors have adapted or changed culturally while living in the United States. Ask them to pinpoint the ways in which they have felt the most pressure to adapt.

ELL Early Advanced Content Tip Review how to read a map and its key as students examine the migration map in the lesson. Ask students to interpret the key using complete sentences, such as *The green arrow shows where people moved between the years A.D. 1 and 1000.*

ELL Activity Review direct and indirect objects. Then have students find and read aloud sentences from the text that relate to *ethnocentrism*. Ask them to identify the direct object (person or thing receiving the action). For example, *British colonists took Aboriginal children.* **(Verbal)**

myWorld Activity   **Step-by-Step Instructions**

 30 min

Before and After

OBJECTIVES

Students will

- identify the effects of colonization on indigenous culture and practices.
- compare and contrast regions' cultural landscapes before and after colonization.

LEARNING STYLE

- Visual

21st Century Learning

- Develop Cultural Awareness

MATERIALS

- Crayons or colored pencils
- Activity Support: Effective Illustrations, p. T17

Activity Steps

1. Tell students that they are going to use information from Section 2 to describe Australia before and after it was settled by Europeans. They will create and share illustrations for an encyclopedia entry about the effects of colonization on Australia, complete with very specific captions.

   L1 Special Needs Use sticky notes representing colonists and Aborigines on maps or projections to help students understand how the British moved from Great Britain to Australia. Ask students to guess what they packed.

2. Distribute *Activity Support: Effective Illustrations.* Tell students to think about and discuss the ways in which the population, culture, land use, and other aspects of Australia changed once European settlers arrived. You might decide to group students according to categories of changes.

3. Have students draw Before and After pictures for the encyclopedia entry. Encourage students to be as specific as possible both in their drawings and their captions. Explain that Before captions should not include information about the After.

   ELL Early Intermediate Provide sentence starters for captions: *Before the British came to Australia, _____. After the British came to Australia, _____.*

   L4 Challenge Tell students to write their captions according to Associated Press (AP) style. Provide guidelines or an online link.

4. Ask each student to present the illustration-caption pair that he or she likes best. Prompt students to comment on the change their classmate is highlighting and all of its possible effects. As an extension, build a class pictorial and digital encyclopedia on colonization with everyone's illustrations.

 More Activities From myWorld Teachers

Local Connections Ask pairs to list what might change in their town if it suddenly became a colony of another town, state, or country. Each partner should choose a list item and create a sign for a class protest on the issue. **(Visual/Verbal)**

Debate and Vote Explain to students that many former U.S. territories have become U.S. states. Have students act as members of Congress and debate whether current U.S. territories in the Pacific region should become states, as in the case of Hawaii. Teach and follow Robert's Rules of Order. **(Logical/Verbal)**

Assimilation Nation? Challenge students to make skits about the process of cultural change dealing either with immigrants in the United States or Aborigines in Australia. **(Kinesthetic/Interpersonal)**

 worldgeography.com (**Teacher Center**) → Find additional resources in the online Teacher Center.

Name _____   Class _____   Date _____

myWorld Activity Support   **Effective Illustrations**

Before and After

Directions Imagine that you have been hired to illustrate an entry in an encyclopedia about Australia. The author wants you to create illustrations that compare and contrast the topics of population, culture, and land use before and after European settlers arrived in Australia. Draw a Before and After picture for one of the topics. Be sure to provide a detailed caption explaining what each picture shows, using information from the section.

Australia: Before Colonization

Caption: _____

_____

_____

Australia: After Colonization

Caption: _____

_____

_____

Name _____ Class _____ Date _____

Enrichment: Cook and the Chronometer

Directions Read the following selection about James Cook and the marine chronometer. Find out how this tool helped him chart, or plot his course, accurately. Then answer the questions below and complete the activity.

What it is Originally, the marine chronometer was similar to an oversized pocket watch. It included special springs that could adjust for changes in temperature. The tool allows sailors to always know the exact time when at sea, despite unpredictable weather and water conditions. Once sailors know the time, they can determine the longitude of their location. Today, sailors use chronometers alongside newer technologies, such as Global Positioning System (GPS) navigation. Modern chronometers use quartz crystals, not springs, to measure time.

Why it was necessary Until British cabinetmaker John Harrison invented the first marine chronometer, sailors were only able to determine the latitude of their location. (To do this, they would measure the altitude of the sun or another star at specific times.) With Harrison's chronometer, sailors could know the correct time of day and use that information to calculate longitude.

How Cook used it James Cook was the first explorer to use a chronometer. He used it during an expedition that left England in 1772. Cook used the chronometer to help him draw accurate maps of New Zealand and Tahiti, as well as several other islands in the south Pacific. His maps gave Europeans a deeper understanding of the Pacific region.

1. What was James Cook able to do with the marine chronometer? What did he create?

   _____
   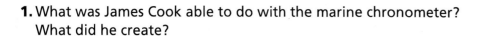

2. How do you think the chronometer affected exploration after Cook?

   _____

3. **Activity** Research a map of the Pacific region that was created during the 1700s or early 1800s. Compare it with a modern-day map of the region and list five differences between the two.

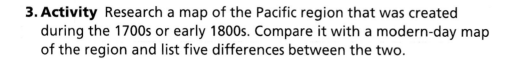

Name _____ Class _____ Date _____

Section Quiz

Directions Answer the following questions using what you learned
in Section 2.

1. _____ Why did the British colonize
Australia and New Zealand?
  a. to enslave native peoples
  b. to use the region's fertile land and
  natural resources
  c. to build new homes for the many
  people who lived in Britain's
  overcrowded cities
  d. to end fighting between native peoples

2. _____ What did British colonists hope to
accomplish by taking Aboriginal children
away from their families?
  a. to assimilate the children into British
  culture
  b. to stop the growth of the Aboriginal
  population
  c. to help Aboriginal families who could
  not feed their children
  d. to learn more about Aboriginal culture

3. _____ The Aborigines were the earliest
people to live in
  a. Polynesia.
  b. New Zealand.
  c. Australia.
  d. Melanesia.

4. _____ The British policy of assimilation
started because of colonists' feelings of
  a. settlement.
  b. poverty.
  c. exploration.
  d. ethnocentrism.

5. _____ What is the main goal of a
missionary?
  a. to settle land
  b. to bring peace to a region
  c. to spread his or her religious beliefs
  d. to help indigenous peoples

6. Fill in the timeline below with at least three major events in
the history of Australia and the Pacific.

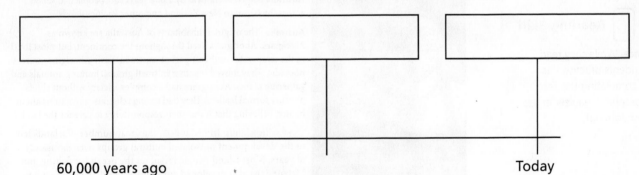

60,000 years ago   Today

History of Australia and the Pacific

- Model preparing to read by previewing the Key Ideas, Key Terms, headings, visuals, and captions. Have students make predictions about what they will learn. For ELL support, post the prompt "I predict I will read about . . ."

- Preview and practice the reading skill, Sequence, by using examples from the early history of your community.

- Teach this section's high-use Academic Vocabulary using the chart on the next page. Have students practice Academic Vocabulary and Key Terms by completing the *Word Wise* page in their **Student Journal.**

GUIDE ON THE SIDE

Migration and Settlement

- **Cause and Effect** How did the geography of Melanesia affect the development of culture? (Since islands are spread apart, cultural groups developed independent of each other and were often isolated.)

- **Predict** How do you think European settlers will adapt to the Aborigines' way of life? (Sample: The Aborigines' life will seem unfamiliar. Europeans were used to European economic and cultural practices.)

 Reading Skill

Sequence While they read, have students practice this skill by completing the *Take Notes* graphic organizer in the **Student Journal.**

Section 2

History of Australia and the Pacific

Key Ideas
- The Pacific region was one of the last places on Earth settled by people.
- By the late 1800s, Australia and the Pacific were under the control of European and other colonial powers.
- Colonization transformed the region.

Key Terms • Aborigines • Maori • assimilation • ethnocentrism • missionary 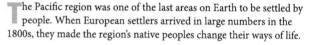 Visual Glossary

 **Reading Skill: Sequence** Take notes using the graphic organizer in your journal.

This Maori woman's chin is marked with the traditional Maori tattoos known as moko. ▼

The Pacific region was one of the last areas on Earth to be settled by people. When European settlers arrived in large numbers in the 1800s, they made the region's native peoples change their ways of life.

Migration and Settlement

People settled the region in three waves of migration, shown on the map in this section. Around 60,000 years ago, the first people settled Australia and New Guinea. By 1,000 years ago, people had sailed across the ocean to New Zealand and other Pacific islands.

Australia The original inhabitants of Australia are known as **Aborigines.** Aborigines lived throughout the continent, but most lived in the temperate southeast part of Australia. Early Aborigines were nomadic. They moved together in small groups, hunting animals and gathering plants. Aborigines had a complex society without chiefs or other formal leaders. They had strong religious convictions about nature, believing that it was their responsibility to care for the land.

The Pacific Islands In Melanesia, the great number of islands led to the development of isolated cultural groups over thousands of years. Most island people relied on the ocean for fishing, but Melanesians also developed agriculture about 10,000 years ago. In Polynesia, kingdoms extended over entire groups of islands.

ACADEMIC VOCABULARY

High-Use Word	Definition and Sample Sentence
exile	*v.* to force out of one's own home *The disgraced politician was exiled from his city.*
strategic	*adj.* important to military or action plans *The candidate's national speech was a strategic moment in her campaign.*

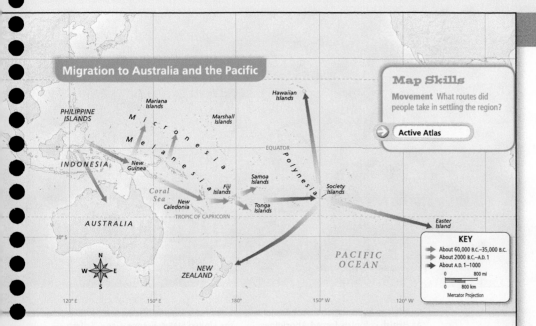

Migration to Australia and the Pacific

Map Skills

Movement What routes did people take in settling the region?

Active Atlas

KEY
About 60,000 B.C.–35,000 B.C.
About 2000 B.C.–A.D. 1
About A.D. 1–1000
0   800 mi
0   800 km
Mercator Projection

Frequent conflict led people to live in protected settlements. Polynesians often went on long-distance ocean trips.

Like other Polynesians, the Maori lived in small settlements. The **Maori** are the original inhabitants of New Zealand and the Cook Islands. The Maori fished, hunted, and farmed. Chiefs were at the top of Maori society. At the bottom of society were slaves, usually captured during warfare.

The center of Maori society is a marae, an enclosed area of land that includes a meeting house and other buildings. Art is an important part of Maori culture. The Maori carve decorations into their buildings, canoes, weapons, and other objects.

Reading Check How did people settle Australia and the Pacific region?

Exploration and Colonization

In the late 1700s, British explorer James Cook claimed Australia and New Zealand for Great Britain. Cook's expeditions increased European interest in the region.

66 In this Extensive Country it can never be doubted but what most sorts of Grain, Fruits, Roots … of every kind would flourish … and here [is food] for more Cattle at all seasons of the year than ever can be brought into this Country. 99

—James Cook, journal entry, 1770

Colonization Begins British settlement of Australia began in 1788. Many early settlers were convicted criminals who had been <u>exiled</u> to Australia. Colonists farmed and ranched. In 1851, colonists discovered gold, and the British population soared.

exile, *v.*, to force out of one's own home

READING CHECK People settled the region in three waves, beginning around 60,000 years ago.

MAP SKILLS People spread south and east from Southeast Asia.

GUIDE ON THE SIDE

- **Identify Details** Where did the Maori live before arriving in New Zealand and the Cook Islands? (Polynesia)

Map Skills Have students examine the map to track settlement in the Pacific region.

- How did patterns of migration change between the three waves? (People began spreading across larger distances, both east and south.)

Exploration and Colonization

- **Identify Details** Reread James Cook's journal excerpt. Which two economic activities did he imagine taking place in Australia and New Zealand? (farming and raising livestock)

Active Atlas

Have students go to myworldgeography.com to further examine maps of Australia and the Pacific.

CULTURE

The Arrival of the Maori Historians now know that people first permanently settled in New Zealand around 1300, arriving from East Polynesia in double-hulled canoes. These canoes have become a major part of Maori culture and tradition. Although legend long stated that the Maori ancestors arrived in a "great fleet" of seven canoes, it is much more likely that tens of canoes made the voyage. Today, Maori tribes trace their origin to individual canoes, or *waka*.

- **Identify Details** Describe the different ways colonizers controlled the Pacific islands. (They governed with colonial governors, military forces, and commercial companies.)

- **Connect** How was the forced transfer of Aboriginal children from their families to white families or institutions an example of ethnocentrism? (Sample: The British thought their culture was better than Aboriginal culture. They hoped to force Aboriginal children to adopt British ways.)

A Changing Region

Lieutenant James Cook was an early British explorer of the region.

British colonization led to conflict with native peoples.

Conflict in Australia and New Zealand As British colonists forced Aborigines off their lands, fighting broke out. In addition, many Aborigines died from European diseases.

The British also practiced forced assimilation. **Assimilation** is the process by which one group takes on the cultural traits of another. British ethnocentrism led settlers to force Aborigines to adopt British customs. **Ethnocentrism** is the attitude that one's own social or cultural group is better than all others. British colonists took Aboriginal children away from their families and forced them to live in institutions or with white families. This practice continued into the 1960s.

British settlers began to arrive in New Zealand in the early 1800s. They were attracted by New Zealand's harbors and fertile soil. Conflict with the Maori led to a series of wars eventually won by Britain.

strategic, *adj.,* important to military or action plans

The Pacific Islands By the early 1900s, the United States, France, Great Britain, and Japan controlled most of the Pacific islands. Colonizers claimed some islands because of their natural resources. Other islands were taken for their location. For example, the Micronesian islands served as a <u>strategic</u> midpoint between the United States and Japan.

Britain ruled its colonies with colonial governors. Other countries controlled their colonies with military forces or through commercial companies.

Colonizers brought many new ideas and customs. For example, colonizers introduced the concept of owning land instead of using land collectively. Some colonizers were **missionaries,** or people sent to another country by a church to spread its religious beliefs.

Reading Check **How did the British treat the region's native people?**

READING CHECK The British tried to control the lives of native peoples, including where they could live.

READING CHECK In most places, the desire for independence was expressed and granted nonviolently.

SECTION 3 ASSESSMENT **1.** British assimilation forced Aborigines to adopt British customs and abandon their own. **2.** Missionaries wanted to spread their religious beliefs. **3.** Countries wanted to make money from the region's land and other natural resources. **4.** Humans came in three waves, starting about 60,000 years

COMMON MISCONCEPTIONS

Guam and the United States Since the United States has so few territories, most students may not understand the U.S. role in Guam and the island's level of independence. Explain that the United States came into possession of Guam following the U.S. victory in the Spanish–American War in 1898. Except for a period of Japanese occupation during World War II, Guam has been under U.S. control ever since. The U.S. military base on the island, used throughout the Vietnam War, remains strategically important to U.S. security.

Guamanians are U.S. citizens but do not vote in American elections. The island's government is led by a popularly elected governor and a 15-seat, one-house legislature. Guam sends a delegate to the House of Representatives. The U.S. president is the official head of state.

Left, Aborigines were forced to adopt British ways. Above, Aborigines protest government policies.

myWorld Activity
Before and After

GUIDE ON THE SIDE

Independence

- **Summarize** Overall, did most of the Pacific region gain its independence peacefully or violently? (peacefully)

- **Categorize** Have Australia and New Zealand broken all ties with Great Britain? (No, they are part of the British Commonwealth of Nations.)

- **Express an Opinion** Are you surprised that the United States still controls part of the Pacific region? Explain. (Sample: Yes. Knowing how the United States fought for its own freedom and for that of other peoples around the world, I am surprised that it would have not have granted independence to its lands in the Pacific; No. The United States government probably thinks these islands are too valuable to give up.)

myWorld Activity

Before and After Find Step-by-Step Instructions and an Activity Support on pp. T16–T17. **(Visual)**

Independence

Australia and New Zealand gained their independence peacefully in the early 1900s. Today, both belong to the British Commonwealth of Nations, which includes many former British colonies.

Most Pacific islands won independence peacefully in the second half of the 1900s. Independence movements played a role on some islands. In Western Samoa (now Samoa), the nonviolent Mau movement worked for independence, which Samoa won in 1962. Still, not all of the Pacific region has been decolonized. The United States, France, and New Zealand still control some Pacific islands.

Reading Check How did the region win independence from colonizers?

Section 2 Assessment

Key Terms
1. How did the British policy of forced assimilation affect Aborigines?
2. What did missionaries to the region seek to do?

Key Ideas
3. Why did countries seek to colonize the region?
4. How did people first settle the region?
5. How did the British colonization of Australia and New Zealand affect native peoples there?

Think Critically
6. **Compare and Contrast** How were the region's people alike and different before British colonization began?
7. **Sequence** In what order were Australia and the three subgroups of Pacific islands settled?

Essential Question
What makes a nation?
8. Does the history of colonization explain the formation of present-day nations in this region? Explain.

ANSWERS

ago. The entire Pacific region was settled by about 1,000 years ago. **5.** Colonization ended up killing many native peoples through war and disease. Those who survived were forced to adopt British ways of life. **6.** Some peoples lived in settlements, and some lived nomadically. Some had their own specific religions. Hunting, fishing, and farming were always important. **7.** Australia and Melanesia were settled first, then Micronesia, and then Polynesia. **8.** The population of the region has changed to include fewer native peoples and more people with a European background.

Aborigines Under British Rule

OBJECTIVES

Students will

- read about the treatment of Aborigines by British settlers.
- learn how the British and Aborigines reacted to changes to Aboriginal culture.
- **ELL** use text-related synonyms to paraphrase lesson content.

SET EXPECTATIONS

In this lesson, students will

- read Aborigines Under British Rule.

1 Connect

Have students describe how they react when someone tells them what to do. Discuss how their reactions differ when the other person is someone they respect. Then discuss what would happen if someone asked them to do something major, like leave their homes. Ask, What would someone else have to do to make you leave your home and neighborhood?

ELL Early Intermediate Have classmates role-play giving and being given directives, some easy and some difficult. Ask students to take turns describing the actions and emotions they see, first in their home language and then in English.

2 Learn

Preview Have students preview pictures and headings. Identify the cultural background of the images. Clarify any questions about the meaning of the defined words by providing examples. Read the introduction.

Read While students read Aborigines Under British Rule, ask questions found in **Guide on the Side** to build understanding of the Key Ideas and objectives.

L3 On-Level Tell partners to write an interview with one of the Aboriginal petitioners. Questions might include, *Who was in charge of your settlement?* or *How is the health of people in the settlement?*

ELL Early Advanced Provide students with a word bank of synonyms of terms in one of

the excerpts, such as *ill* for *sick* or *legal* for *lawful*. Ask them to describe the excerpt using words in the word bank.

myWorld Activity: In Your Own Three Words Discuss both sources in the feature with students, prompting them to assume different viewpoints and audiences. Then have them cut out and complete the cards on *Activity Support: Description Cards*, describing each card topic in only three words. Arrange students in pairs. Have partners take turns looking at the words on each other's cards and guessing the description on the other side. Work with students to make a list of common words and then discuss why they think these words were suggested so often. **(Verbal)**

⏱ 20 min

3 Understand

Review Have students draw a cumulative class illustration of the effects of European colonization on the Aborigines or tell a cumulative class story about it, one person at a time. Continue until all of the information in the feature is represented.

Assess Have students write their responses to the Assessment questions in their notebooks.

Ask additonal questions using the highlighted vocabulary in the feature.

Remediate If students struggle with the wording of the Aboriginal Protection Act, help them rewrite or paraphrase parts. Then ask students to sort what the British do want to happen from what they do not want to happen.

Name _____ Class _____ Date _____

 myWorld Activity Support   Description Cards

In Your Own Three Words

Directions Think about what you have learned about relations between Aborigines and British settlers in Section 2 and the Primary Source feature. Then cut out the four cards below. On the back of each card, write three words that fit the category on the front. You may use nouns, verbs, or adjectives. When you have finished your cards, show each set of words to your partner and have him or her guess which category they describe.

Three words that describe Flinders Island	Three words that describe the Aboriginal Protection Act
Three words that describe the needs of Aborigines in the 1800s	Three words that describe the needs of British settlers in the 1800s

T21

HISTORY

Flinders Island After years of fighting with British settlers in what came to be known as the "Black War," the Aborigines who remained in modern-day Tasmania (known as Van Diemen's Land at the time) agreed to relocate to northern Tasmania with the understanding that they would be allowed to live peacefully. Yet the Wybalenna settlement at Flinders Island turned out to be far from peaceful. Aborigines were forced to adopt Christian beliefs and European ways, and their health and food needs were frequently ignored. More than 100 Wybalenna settlers died from malnutrition and disease.

GUIDE ON THE SIDE

Compare Viewpoints Help students identify the "voice" behind each source. Use the introduction to present the relevant groups, Aborigines and British officials.

ANSWERS

A It has shrunk.

B Sample: He is neglectful, only treating people when they are very sick. He manipulates food rations and uses imprisonment to get what he wants from the Aborigines.

C Sample: They may have thought of them as an easy solution to getting Aborigines out of the way and freeing up more land for European settlement. Officials may not have paid much attention to conditions at the settlements.

Primary Source

Aborigines Under British Rule

Key Idea
• When Britain colonized Australia, British settlers forced Aborigines off their lands and took control of many aspects of their lives.

The British settlement of Australia increased rapidly in the 1800s. British officials often forced Aborigines to give up their lands to colonists. They sometimes made Aborigines adopt British customs and live on settlements controlled by British officials. Living conditions in these settlements are described in a letter written by a group of Aborigines to Britain's Queen Victoria in 1846. British officials also passed laws that gave themselves the power to control Aborigines' lives. These excerpts will help you understand how Aborigines and British officials interacted in the 1800s.

▲ British officials and soldiers interacting with Aborigines, about 1790

Aborigines in the 1800s ▼

Read the text on the right. Stop at each circled letter. Then answer the question with the same letter on the left.

A Summarize How has the population of the Aborigines' community changed?

B Paraphrase In your own words, explain how the British official treated the Aborigines.

C Infer How do you think British officials felt about the Aboriginal settlements they created?

vermin, *n.*, animal pests, especially insects
rations, *n.*, food allowances

Petition to Queen Victoria

❝ [W]hen we left our own place we **A** were plenty of People, we are now but a little one … Our houses were let fall down [and] they were never cleaned but were covered with **B** vermin … We were often without Clothes … [and the settlement's British official] did not care to mind us when we were sick until we were very bad. Eleven of us died when he was here. He put many of us into Jail … because we would not be his **C** slaves. He kept us from our Rations when he pleased [and] sometimes gave us bad Rations of Tea [and] Tobacco. ❞

—Aborigines on Flinders Island, Tasmania, Australia, 1846

ANALYZE THE DOCUMENTS 1. Since the petition was made more than 20 years before the Aboriginal Protection Act was passed, it is obvious that the attitudes and interests that inspired the act—such as desires to regulate Aboriginal contracts and labor—existed long before they were made part of legislation. **2.** Students' poems should reflect upon the loss of Aboriginal cultural opportunities and connections with tribal lands from the time the Aborigines were forced to relocate and adapt to European

21st Century Learning COMPARE VIEWPOINTS

To help students compare viewpoints while reading both excerpts, first have them come up with a list of the emotions they think Aborigines and British officials must have felt when writing and reading each source. Then read each excerpt twice, telling students to first listen to it as if they are Aborigines and then as if they are British settlers. Discuss the differences in how they felt when hearing the petition and the act. Encourage them to use information they learned in Section 2 to support their descriptions.

Read the text on the right. Stop at each circled letter. Then answer the question with the same letter on the left.

D Identify What is the governor able to do?

E Paraphrase In your own words, explain the governor's powers over Aborigines.

F Analyze Why do you think British officials wanted to control Aborigines' labor and earnings?

prescribe, *v.*, to choose, decide
reside, *v.*, to live
exertions, *n.*, work
apportion, *v.*, to divide, distribute

Aboriginal Protection Act

D " It shall be lawful for the Governor from time to time to make regulations and orders for any of the purposes hereinafter mentioned ...
(I.) For prescribing the place where any aboriginal or any tribe of aborigines shall reside.

E (II.) For prescribing the terms on which contracts for and on behalf of aboriginals may be made with Europeans, and upon which certificates may be granted to aboriginals who may be able and willing to earn a living by their own exertions.
(III.) For apportioning amongst aboriginals the earnings of

F aboriginals under any contract, or where aboriginals are located on a reserve, the net produce of the labor of such aboriginals. "
—Victoria, Australia, Act of Parliament, 1869

Aboriginal children were sometimes taken away from their homes. ▼

An Aboriginal man examining a rock painting ▼

GUIDE ON THE SIDE

ANSWERS

D The governor can make laws and then change them.

E Sample: The governor can tell individual Aborigines or Aboriginal tribes where they must live. He can also control the business relationships between Aborigines and settlers.

F Sample: They did not want to have to pay Aborigines much for their work or land, but wanted to protect themselves from complaints.

Analyze the Documents

1. **Synthesize** Explain how the 1846 petition shows that British attempts to control Aborigines existed long before the 1869 Aboriginal Protection Act.

2. **Writing Task** Examine the two documents. How do you think Aboriginal culture and society were affected by British treatment? Explain in a poem.

culture. Poems may include examples of losses, such as fluency in native languages.

Australia and the Pacific Today

OBJECTIVES

Students will know

- characteristics of different cultures and environments within the Pacific region.
- similarities and differences between regional governments and economies.

Students will be able to

- identify main ideas and details that describe the Pacific region's culture.
- generate new ideas about environmental changes in the Pacific region.

SET EXPECTATIONS

In this section, students will

- read Australia and the Pacific Today.
- predict how growing environmental problems might affect various groups.
- go On Assignment in Australia and the Pacific.

CORE CONCEPTS

You may wish to teach or reteach the following lessons from the Core Concepts Handbook:

- Water and Climate, p. 36
- People's Impact on the Environment, p. 52
- Political Systems, p. 106

KEY

Differentiated Instruction	English Language Instruction
L1 Special Needs **L2** Extra Support	**ELL** Beginner **ELL** Early Intermediate **ELL** Intermediate
L3 On-Level **L4** Challenge	**ELL** Early Advanced **ELL** Advanced

1 Connect
Make learning meaningful

Make Connections Remind students of Jack Terei's story in the chapter opener. Ask them if, like Jack, some of their school or extracurricular activities connect to their cultural background, either directly or indirectly. Ask for examples.

ELL Intermediate Suggest and demonstrate common comparison words, such as *similarly, likewise, both,* and *just as.*

Activate Prior Knowledge Prompt students to recall what they learned about the treatment of the Aborigines and Maori in the previous section. Create a class list of words to describe these peoples' quality of life under colonization. Ask students to predict what kind of long-term effects this treatment may have had on living standards and population.

L2 Extra Support Review the events described in Section 2. Have students identify periods when the future success of the Aborigine and Maori people may have been affected the most, such as during early colonization.

Prepare Follow the steps in the section **Preview.** Preteach the Key Terms. Then have students complete *Word Wise* in their **Student Journal** using in-text clues and the glossary for help.

2 Experience
Teach knowledge and skills

Read Use **Background** notes and **Guide on the Side** questions to model active reading. Have students use *Take Notes* in their **Student Journal** to identify main ideas and details about culture, economy, government, and the environment in Australia and the Pacific today. Have students complete **21st Century Online Tutor** *Identify Main Ideas and Details* and apply this skill to reading the section.

L2 Extra Support Have students create three-column tables in their notes that include details from the reading about the economies of Australia, New Zealand, and the other Pacific islands. Later, use color coding to distinguish primary and secondary industries.

ELL Early Intermediate/Intermediate Help students phonetically break down the Key Terms, especially those with potentially confusing silent consonants, including *coup* and *drought.* Use the **Online Student Edition** for audio samples.

Practice: myWorld Activity Students will brainstorm the narrow and broad implications of environmental problems in the Pacific region, representing affected groups in a town meeting. **Step-by-Step Instructions** and **More Activities** follow on pp. T24–T25.

SECTION 3 RESOURCE GUIDE

FOR THE STUDENT

my worldgeography.com Student Center

- Language Lesson
- Culture Close-up
- Data Discovery

Student Edition (print and online)

- Australia and the Pacific Today

Student Journal (print and online)

- Section 3 Word Wise
- Section 3 Take Notes

21st Century Learning Online Tutor

- Identify Main Ideas and Details
- Generate New Ideas

FOR THE TEACHER

my worldgeography.com Teacher Center

- Online Lesson Planner
- Presentations for Projection
- SuccessTracker

ProGuide: Australia and the Pacific

- Lesson Plan, pp. T22–T23
- myWorld Activity Step-by-Step Instructions, p. T24
- Activity Support: Position Statements, p. T25
- myWorld Geography Enrichment, p. T26
- Section Quiz, p. T27

Accelerating the Progress of ELLs

- Organizing Information Strategies, p. 48

3 Understand
Assess understanding

Review Review students' work in their **Student Journal**.

Assess Knowledge and Skills Use the Section Assessment and Section Quiz to check students' progress.

Assess Understanding Review students' responses to the Section Assessment Essential Question prompt.

Remediate Use these strategies to review and remediate.

If students struggle to . . .	Try these strategies.
Understand the role of the British monarch in Australia's and New Zealand's governments	Review the structure of monarchies and democracies in Core Concepts Lesson 8.2.
Appreciate the impact of climate change	Have students read *Enrichment: Disappearing Reefs.*
Identify economic features of specific regions	Create a chart that answers *What do we make or grow?* and *How do we get what we do not make or grow?* for the region.

ELL Support

ELL Objective Students will conjugate English verbs to describe content.

Cultural Connections Have students explain in their home languages and through anecdotes the connection, if present, between ethnicity and standard of living in a familiar country or communities.

ELL Intermediate Content Tip Review the content under the Economy heading. Have students take turns using first person, second person, and third person to describe a single regional economic concept. Sample sentences: *You make money from farming in New Zealand. He makes money by fishing, a primary industry in the Pacific Islands.*

ELL Activity Use pieces of string to model the concept of *long* and *short,* including in terms of time, with students. Then have groups role-play and verbally describe not eating for 10 minutes, then one hour, and so on. Help them label their descriptions as *long-term effect* and *short-term effect.* **(Visual/Verbal)**

myWorld Activity Step-by-Step Instructions

 30 min

Take Action on the Pacific Environment

OBJECTIVES
Students will
- express opinions about how different communities are affected by environmental problems.
- generate creative, new ideas about how to solve environmental conflicts and why action is necessary.

LEARNING STYLE
- Verbal

21st Century Learning
- Generate New Ideas

MATERIALS
- Activity Support: Position Statements, p. T25

Activity Steps

1. Tell students that they are going to use what they have learned about environmental dangers in Australia and the Pacific to help voice the need for change. Working within a small group, they will brainstorm how climate change may be affecting different groups in the region. Groups will then meet as a class to participate in a "town meeting" about the issue.

2. Divide students into groups of four. Tell students they have 15 minutes to brainstorm the ramifications of each problem described on *Activity Support: Position Statements*. When they have finished brainstorming, each student should be assigned or choose to represent one of the four problems at the meeting.

    L2 Extra Support Tell students to find at least one sentence in Section 3 that relates to each problem on the worksheet. Have them rewrite the sentences in their own words and share them with the rest of the group.

3. Write the town meeting agenda on the board. There should be at least one item for each issue from Activity Support such as *Item 1: Relief for farmers, Item 2: Native plants in danger, Item 3: Lowland dangers,* and *Item 4: Overfishing problems.*

4. As you proceed through the agenda, the students connected to each item should stand and speak about how the environmental issue is affecting "their" lives and others. Students should also be prepared to suggest a solution.

    ELL Intermediate Give students a scaffold for arguments. For example, students could speak at the meeting by starting with *If _____ does not stop, then my family will have to _____,* or *_____ is a problem because it can hurt_____.*

More Activities From myWorld Teachers

Local Connections Ask students to make a poster charting primary industries in the region and their connections to local culture, such as business names, regional nicknames and cuisine, or annual festivals. **(Visual)**

Culture Debate Post this sentence: *The Internet and traditional culture do not go hand in hand.* Then tell students that Internet usage is on the rise in many formerly isolated islands. In New Caledonia the percentage of Internet users rose from 14 percent in 2000 to 33.2 percent in 2007. Have pairs take opposite sides and debate the statement. **(Interpersonal)**

Nuclear Research Have students research which Pacific islands were previously used for nuclear testing. Tell them to create informational flyers, complete with maps, that describe the resulting concerns. **(Verbal)**

 worldgeography.com (Teacher Center) → Find additional resources in the online Teacher Center.

Name _____ Class _____ Date _____

myWorld Activity Support   **Position Statements**

Take Action on the Pacific Environment

Directions Work with your group to brainstorm ideas about who the following environmental issues affect and how. Complete the table with short- and long-term effects of the different issues. Then write a possible solution to one issue at the bottom of the page. Use your notes to participate in a class town meeting.

Issue	People Affected	Short-Term Effects	Long-Term Effects
1: Drought is making it impossible to grow the desired amount of crops.			
2: New construction is putting endangered species at higher risk.			
3: Rising sea levels are eroding land both near and away from the coast.			
4: Overfishing has led to fewer fish and other marine life.			

For Issue _____, I propose the following solution: _____

_____

_____

_____

_____

_____

Name _____ Class _____ Date _____

Enrichment: Disappearing Reefs

Directions Read the selection below. Answer the questions that follow and complete the activity.

One of the most alarming environmental problems in the Pacific region today is the disappearance of coral reefs. Scientists estimate that reefs in both the Pacific and Indian Oceans have been dying at a rate of almost 600 square miles a year since the late 1960s.

The effect of this problem spans the Pacific region. Many tourism businesses that depend on the reefs have had to close. Some islands' food supplies have been reduced, as fish that live in reefs are no longer able to hide from predators.

What is causing so many reefs to die in the Pacific? Researchers point to a number of factors. First, warmer ocean temperatures—believed to be the result of climate change—are making it more difficult for the tiny plant-like organisms living in reefs to stay there. When these organisms leave a reef, the coral's food and oxygen supplies are reduced. Warmer waters also seem to weaken reefs' immune systems, or the way that they keep themselves healthy. In addition, the water in the Pacific Ocean has been growing more acidic in recent years. Acidic chemicals slow coral growth and recovery. Finally, a wide range of human activities in the region have hurt Pacific reefs. For example, fishing boats sometimes use dynamite near reefs to stun fish and bring them to the surface. Also, topsoil runoff from deforestation can smother, or completely cover, coral reefs.

Australia, New Zealand, and other Pacific islands have begun working on programs that will keep coral reefs healthy. For example, in Samoa and American Samoa, some reefs have been officially named protected reserves. Yet the nations of the Pacific region know that it will take bigger changes to keep the reefs from dying.

1. What are some of the reasons behind the loss of coral reefs?

_____

2. In what ways does the disappearance of coral reefs show human dependence on the environment and vice versa?

_____

3. Activity Conduct research to identify one of the nations in the Pacific region that has lost a large amount of coral reefs. On a map of this nation, mark areas of industry or other economic activity (such as farming or tree clearing) that you believe may be directly or indirectly harming reefs.

Name _____ Class _____ Date _____

Section Quiz

Directions Answer the following questions using what you learned
in Section 3.

1. _____ Why are Australian Aborigines an
   example of indigenous people?
   a. They were already living in Australia
      when European settlers arrived.
   b. They were not yet living in Australia
      when European settlers arrived.
   c. They arrived in Australia only recently.
   d. They do not actually live in Australia.

2. _____ Which of the following is an example
   of a primary industry?
   a. shipping
   b. mining
   c. manufacturing
   d. telecommunications

3. _____ Which of the following adjectives
   accurately describes nuclear weapons?
   a. destructive
   b. gentle
   c. harmless
   d. untested

4. _____ What is one possible cause of climate
   change?
   a. tornadoes
   b. famine
   c. drought
   d. pollution

5. _____ How have some Pacific island
   governments been affected by coups?
   a. The governments have helped organize
      the coups.
   b. The governments have disappeared
      altogether.
   c. The governments have been overthrown
      by the military.
   d. The governments have all grown as
      stable as Australia's government.

6. What are the reasons that so many cultures exist in the Pacific
   islands? Predict whether this diversity will increase, decrease, or
   remain about the same. Support your prediction.

   _____

   _____

   _____

   _____

   _____

   _____

Australia and the Pacific Today

- Model preparing to read by previewing the Key Ideas, Key Terms, headings, visuals, and captions. Have students make predictions about what they will learn. For ELL support, post the prompt "I predict I will read about . . ."

- Preview and practice the reading skill, Identify Main Ideas and Details, by using examples about the economy of your community.

- Teach this section's high-use Academic Vocabulary using the chart on the next page. Have students practice Academic Vocabulary and Key Terms by completing the *Word Wise* page in their **Student Journal.**

GUIDE ON THE SIDE

People and Culture

- **Draw Conclusions** Look at the physical map of the Pacific region in Section 1. Why do you think so many Asians have immigrated to Australia? (Asia is the continent closest to Australia.)

- **Infer** How do you think Aboriginal Australians reacted to the government's 2008 apology? (Sample: Many Aborigines probably thought that the apology was issued too late; other Aborigines may have appreciated the idea of the apology but wanted to see actions to back up the words.)

Reading Skill

Identify Main Ideas and Details While they read, have students practice this skill by completing the *Take Notes* graphic organizer in the **Student Journal.**

 Culture Close-up

Coober Pedy, South Australia, is often called the "opal capital of the world." Have students investigate the town's mines, some of which now function as homes and churches.

Section **3**

Australia and the Pacific Today

Key Ideas
- The region has a great deal of cultural diversity.
- Countries in the region have different forms of government and different levels of economic development.
- Protecting the environment is a major concern for the region's people.

Key Terms • indigenous • coup • secondary industry • primary industry • drought • climate change • nuclear weapon

Visual Glossary

Reading Skill: Identify Main Ideas and Details Take notes using the graphic organizer in your journal.

Most Australians, such as the man below, are descended from British settlers. ▼

 Culture Close-up

Australia and the Pacific region are home to many cultures and ethnic groups, such as Jack's Maori people in New Zealand. A shared history and a blend of different cultures and traditions have shaped life in the region. Today, Australia and New Zealand are wealthy, highly developed nations with modern industrial economies. The smaller Pacific islands are less developed, with economies based largely on tourism and the use of natural resources.

People and Culture

Australia, New Zealand, and the Pacific islands include people from many different ethnic groups and cultures. As a result, the population of the region is diverse.

Australia and New Zealand Most Australians and New Zealanders have British ancestors. Since the 1970s, growing numbers of Asians and Pacific islanders have moved to these two countries.

Smaller numbers of Australians and New Zealanders are descended from **indigenous** people, or people native to the region. Only about 1 percent of Australia's 22 million people are Aboriginal. As you learned in Section 2, British settlers and the Australian government mistreated Aborigines for many years. In 2008, the Australian government officially apologized for this unjust treatment of Aborigines.

ACADEMIC VOCABULARY

High-Use Word	Definition and Sample Sentence
compensate	*v.* to pay *The business owner compensated her employees for their labor.*
corruption	*n.* improper use of power *Paying someone to vote a certain way is an example of corruption.*

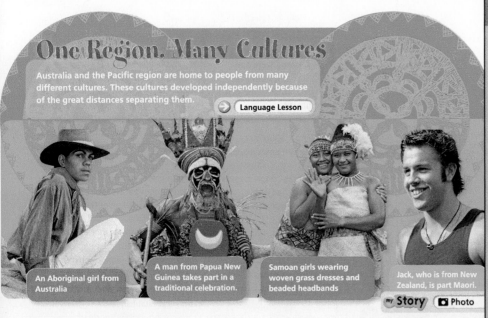

One Region, Many Cultures

Australia and the Pacific region are home to people from many different cultures. These cultures developed independently because of the great distances separating them.

Language Lesson

An Aboriginal girl from Australia

A man from Papua New Guinea takes part in a traditional celebration.

Samoan girls wearing woven grass dresses and beaded headbands

Jack, who is from New Zealand, is part Maori.

my Story   Photo

New Zealand has a larger population of indigenous people: about 8 percent of New Zealand's 4 million people are Maori. Like the Aborigines, the Maori were forced to adopt many British ways of life. Still, Maori culture has survived. In recent years, Maori people have gained more political power. Since the 1970s, the New Zealand government has paid hundreds of millions of dollars to Maori groups to <u>compensate</u> them for having taken Maori land in the past.

In general, Australians and New Zealanders are healthy and well educated, with long average life expectancies. However, many Aborigines and Maori have lower standards of living and levels of education than other Australians and New Zealanders. Government leaders are working to improve the political and economic status of indigenous peoples.

Pacific Islands Over time, Pacific islanders developed many different languages, religions, and customs. European colonization reduced this cultural diversity. For example, Pacific people once practiced hundreds of different religions. Today, most are Christian. Still, most Pacific islanders are indigenous people.

Although modern culture has spread throughout the region, some islanders have kept traditional customs. For example, many Pacific islanders practice traditional forms of art, dance, and music.

Reading Check What is the name of New Zealand's indigenous people?

compensate, *v.*, pay

READING CHECK The Maori are New Zealand's indigenous people.

GUIDE ON THE SIDE

- **Identify Details** Where do indigenous people make up a larger percentage of the population, Australia or New Zealand? (New Zealand)

- **Synthesize** How have Pacific islanders managed to remain true to parts of their native culture even after years of European influence? (They have continued to practice many of their own traditions, such as dance, art, and music.)

- **Infer** Why do you think indigenous people in Australia and New Zealand have a lower standard of living? (Sample: For years, indigenous people were treated as a lower class by European colonists and denied opportunities. Now they must struggle to overcome years of oppression.)

Language Lesson

Have students go to myworldgeography.com, where Jack will teach them how to say greetings in Te Reo Maori.

PRIMARY SOURCE

Apology to Aborigines Discuss with students the following excerpt from the second half of Australian Prime Minister Kevin Rudd's 2008 formal apology to Aborigines. Ask, What does the prime minister hope the apology will achieve? What specific issues does he mention?

"We today take this first step by acknowledging the past and laying claim to a future that embraces all Australians. A future where this Parliament resolves that the injustices of the past must never, never happen again. A future where we harness the determination of all Australians, Indigenous and non-Indigenous, to close the gap that lies between us in life expectancy, educational achievement and economic opportunity . . . A future where all Australians, whatever their origins, are truly equal partners, with equal opportunities."

Government

- **Infer** Why do you think coups take place? (Some people are not satisfied with the current government.)

- **Compare and Contrast** How are the governments of Australia and New Zealand similar and different? (Both are parliamentary democracies; their citizens have similar rights and responsibilities; Australia is divided into six states, but New Zealand does not have any provinces or states.)

Analyze Visuals Have students examine the three photos and their captions.

- Are you surprised to learn that the British monarch still plays a role in Australia's government? Explain. (Sample: No, I am not surprised. A large percentage of Australia's population is descended from British citizens, and those people probably do not mind having some connections to Great Britain.)

Government

Australia and New Zealand were once British colonies. As a result, both have governments that are similar to the British system of government.

Australia and New Zealand Australia and New Zealand are parliamentary democracies. In these systems, citizens elect representatives to a parliament, or legislature. The parliament then chooses a prime minister as the head of the government. The prime minister and the parliament govern the country.

Australia has six states. As in the United States, these states have a great deal of power to govern themselves. They also have their own legislatures and court systems. New Zealand does not have any provinces or states, but it does have local and regional governments.

Citizens of Australia and New Zealand have rights and responsibilities similar to those of U.S. citizens. For example, Australians have freedom of religion and freedom of speech. There are also differences. Australians who are registered to vote can be fined for failing to vote, for example.

Pacific Islands The Pacific islands have a variety of governments, although most are democratic. A few of these countries have suffered from political <u>corruption</u> or unstable governments. For example, Fiji's military has led four coups since 1987. A **coup** is the sudden, violent overthrow of a government, often by the military.

Reading Check How does Australia select leaders and establish laws?

corruption, *n.,* improper use of power

Queen Elizabeth II of the United Kingdom is the official head of state of Australia, New Zealand, and several other former British colonies. She has little real power, however. ▼

Pacific Governments

Many of the region's countries are parliamentary democracies. Above, a Papua New Guinea man waits to vote in a national election. Left, Australia's Parliament

READING CHECK Australians elect their leaders. These leaders help establish law by working in or with the parliament.

ECONOMY

New Zealand Sheep Farming For many decades, sheep farming dominated New Zealand's economy, resulting in about 20 sheep for every one New Zealander. Sheep wool and meat made up the most important industry from 1856 to 1987, dropping in the 1990s as dairy farming increased. In 1982, New Zealand was home to 70 million sheep; in 2007, there were 39 million.

The country's varied landscape has led to the cultivation of several breeds, some of which do better in highlands, some of whom are better suited to the hill country, and some that thrive in the lowlands. European settlers first raised sheep on the drier, eastern side of South Island, gradually expanding to wetter North Island as the Maori living there lost more of their land.

Economy

The region's levels of economic development vary greatly. While Australia and New Zealand have highly developed market economies, most smaller Pacific islands have developing economies.

Australia and New Zealand Australia's major industries are agriculture, mining, tourism, and manufacturing. Although Australia exports natural resources to many countries in Asia, many Australian businesses are secondary industries. A **secondary industry** involves the use of resources to create new products, as occurs in manufacturing. Australia's highly educated population and advanced technology have helped its industries modernize and succeed. As a result, Australia has a wealthy economy with a high economic output per person.

New Zealand's economy is similar to Australia's, although it is smaller. Services, industry, and tourism are the most valuable elements of New Zealand's economy. New Zealand farmers raise cows and sheep for meat, dairy, and wool products.

Pacific Islands Many island economies rely on primary industries such as fishing. A **primary industry** involves the collection of resources from nature. Agriculture and fishing are important primary industries.

Many islands have joined together in trade and business groups, such as the Pacific Islands Forum. By working together, islanders hope that they can attract international business and tourism to their islands, improving their economies and standards of living.

Reading Check Which countries in the region are wealthiest?

my World IN NUMBERS
The region's countries catch about **1.4** million fish per year—less than **1%** of the world's total fish catch.

Sydney, Australia ▼

Output by Economic Sector

Australia: 2.5%, 26.4%, 71.1%

Solomon Islands: 42%, 47%, 11%

Agriculture Industry Services
SOURCE: CIA World Factbook

Chart Skills
The region's economies vary widely. How do the economies of Australia and the Solomon Islands differ?

Data Discovery

CHART SKILLS Australia's economy relies much more heavily on service industries. The Solomon Islands rely more heavily on agriculture than Australia.

READING CHECK Australia and New Zealand are the wealthiest countries, while the economies of most of the smaller islands are still developing.

ANSWERS

Economy

- **Identify Main Ideas** How does the size of a country seem to be related to the size of its economy? (In the Pacific region, smaller countries typically have smaller economies.)

- **Synthesize** How is the role of natural resources different in primary and secondary industries? Give examples. (In a primary industry, the natural resource is collected to make money, such as with fishing. In a secondary industry, the natural resource is used to create a new product, such as making steel from iron and other metals.)

Chart Skills Have students use the two circle graphs to compare economy size.

- Explain the role of industry in both economies. (Industry is important in both economies, although it is much more important in Australia than in the Solomon Islands.)

Data Discovery

Have students visit myworldgeography.com to see more data about life in the region.

GEOGRAPHY

Disappearing Species While some Pacific islands are worried about disappearing land, Australia is worried about disappearing species. As one of the 17 countries in the world labeled "megadiverse"—places taking up less than 10 percent of global surface but accounting for more than 70 percent of biological life—Australia is home to a vast number of species, of which 84 percent of plant species, 83 percent of mammal species, and 45 percent of birds are found only on that continent.

As a result of the relatively recent and rapid settlement of Australia, more than 50 animal species and 60 plant species have become extinct since European settlement. Conservation and protection of endangered species are now a primary focus of the Australian government, which works with state, territory, and local governments to identify threatened species and take steps to protect suffering habitats.

GUIDE ON THE SIDE

Closer Look

Disappearing Islands

- Look at the map. How will Tuvalu be different in 2100? (Much of its northern land will have disappeared beneath the ocean's surface.)

- How is the rise in sea levels a different kind of environmental problem than others you know about? (Sample: There might be little humans can do to prevent it.)

myWorld Activity

Take Action on the Pacific Environment Find Step-by-Step Instructions and an Activity Support on pp. T24–T25. **(Verbal)**

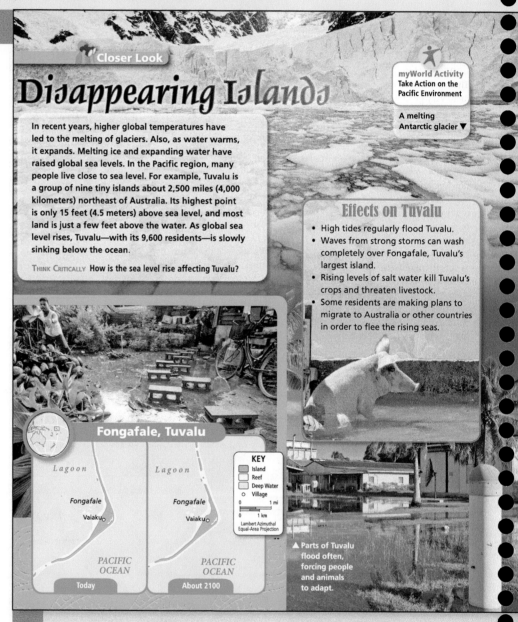

Closer Look

Disappearing Islands

myWorld Activity
Take Action on the Pacific Environment

A melting Antarctic glacier ▼

In recent years, higher global temperatures have led to the melting of glaciers. Also, as water warms, it expands. Melting ice and expanding water have raised global sea levels. In the Pacific region, many people live close to sea level. For example, Tuvalu is a group of nine tiny islands about 2,500 miles (4,000 kilometers) northeast of Australia. Its highest point is only 15 feet (4.5 meters) above sea level, and most land is just a few feet above the water. As global sea level rises, Tuvalu—with its 9,600 residents—is slowly sinking below the ocean.

THINK CRITICALLY How is the sea level rise affecting Tuvalu?

Effects on Tuvalu

- High tides regularly flood Tuvalu.
- Waves from strong storms can wash completely over Fongafale, Tuvalu's largest island.
- Rising levels of salt water kill Tuvalu's crops and threaten livestock.
- Some residents are making plans to migrate to Australia or other countries in order to flee the rising seas.

Fongafale, Tuvalu

Lagoon

Fongafale

Vaiaku

Today

Lagoon

Fongafale

Vaiaku

About 2100

KEY
- Island
- Reef
- Deep Water
- ○ Village

0   1 mi
0   1 km
Lambert Azimuthal
Equal-Area Projection

PACIFIC OCEAN

PACIFIC OCEAN

▲ Parts of Tuvalu flood often, forcing people and animals to adapt.

THINK CRITICALLY Rising sea level is causing Tuvalu to lose land.

READING CHECK Sea level rise is causing erosion in low-lying areas.

SECTION 3 ASSESSMENT 1. Climate change may be responsible for a rise in sea level, causing countries in the region to lose land. **2.** Primary industries collect natural resources. Secondary industries use these resources to make products. **3.** The environment often determines where and how the region's people will live and make money. **4.** Australia and New Zealand have large economies. Most other

HISTORY

Bikini Atoll One of the most notorious nuclear testing grounds in the Pacific islands is Bikini Atoll. Between 1946 and 1958, while under the administration of the U.S. Navy and before it became part of the Marshall Islands, this group of approximately 20 small coral islands became the site of Operation Crossroads. An experiment that tested the effects of both airborne and underwater nuclear bombs on naval vessels, the operation required 167 indigenous people to leave the islands. In 1956, a U.S. plane dropped a hydrogen bomb on the atoll.

Decades later, radioactivity levels remain dangerously high on Bikini Atoll, making U.S. efforts at resettlement impossible. After a lawsuit was brought against the United States in the 1980s by Bikini islanders, U.S. clean-up efforts began, the first of which was completed in 1998. Today, some tourist activity, including diving, is allowed.

Environment

Pacific economies often depend on the environment. For example, tourism relies on the region's sandy beaches and clear blue water. Agriculture and fishing involve the use of natural resources. Today, people are working to protect the environment and use resources carefully. But the Pacific region still faces environmental challenges.

Drought Australia is the driest inhabited continent. In recent years, many areas of the country have been affected by drought. A **drought** is a long period of extremely dry weather. Drought has caused Australia's farms to produce fewer and smaller harvests.

Climate Change Climate change is another major environmental problem. **Climate change** is a long-term, significant change to a region's average weather. Natural processes can cause climate change. However, many scientists believe that human activity—such as air pollution—is a major factor.

Perhaps the most important effect of climate change in the Pacific region is a rise in sea level. This rise is caused by the melting of glaciers and the warming and expansion of water due to higher global temperatures. Many scientists believe that the sea level will continue to rise in coming years, perhaps by as much as two feet or more by 2100.

Since many of the people in the Pacific region live near sea level, the sea level rise is a serious concern. Even a small rise can affect low-lying areas. Storms can push higher water farther onto land, causing widespread erosion.

Other Issues Some economic activities can cause environmental harm. For example, mining can cause water and soil pollution. In addition, the United States, France, and the United Kingdom tested nuclear weapons in the region from the 1940s to the 1990s. A **nuclear weapon** is a powerful explosive device that can cause widespread destruction. This testing may have harmful long-term effects on the region's people and ecosystems.

Reading Check How is sea level rise affecting the Pacific region?

Section 3 Assessment

Key Terms
1. How is climate change affecting Australia and the Pacific region?
2. What are primary and secondary industries?

Key Ideas
3. Why are the region's people concerned about the environment?
4. Describe the region's economies.
5. Why does the region have such a wide variety of cultures?

Think Critically
6. **Summarize** Summarize the present-day conditions of Australia's indigenous people.
7. **Draw Conclusions** Why might people who live on an island be able to preserve their culture for a long time without change?

Essential Question
What makes a nation?
8. How do governments and economies vary among the region's nations?

The Economy of the Pacific Islands

OBJECTIVES

Students will

- compare features of the past and present Pacific island economies.
- describe the ways in which the Pacific islands plan to grow their economies in the future.
- **ELL** use comparative adjectives to describe economy sizes.

SET EXPECTATIONS

In this case study, students will

- read The Economy of the Pacific Islands.
- calculate and examine GDP per capita in the activity *How Much Per Person?*

---

1 Connect

Ask students to think about personal skills that they might be able to use to be successful as adults (for example, writing talent, athleticism, knowledge of non-English languages). Then tell them to think of these skills as "resources." Discuss creative ways to turn these resources into something bigger, such as starting a business (self-promotional skills) or becoming a doctor (good listening skills), and what would be required to do this.

L1 Special Needs Ask students to list ways to complete the statement *I am really good at _____*. Have students list several items, pick one, and explain how it helps them in life.

---

2 Learn

Preview Have students preview pictures and headings. Remind them of what they have already read of the differences between natural resources in Australia and New Zealand and in the Pacific islands.

Read While students read The Economy of the Pacific Islands, ask questions found in **Guide on the Side** to build understanding of Key Ideas and objectives.

L2 Extra Support Give students the following scaffolds to reinforce comprehension: *In the past, Pacific Island economies were _____. Today, the economies are _____. In the future, Pacific Island economies will hopefully _____.*

myWorld Activity: How Much per Person? Remind students that a nation's Gross Domestic Product (GDP) is the value of all goods and services produced there within a specific year. Tell them to use *Activity Support: GDP Calculator* (with a calculator, if desired) to calculate the GDP per capita (or per person) in the Pacific islands listed in the table and then answer related questions. Ask for hypotheses on the connection between land area and GDP. **(Logical)**

20 min

ELL Early Intermediate Help students use comparative adjectives to describe the different sizes of Pacific economies. Review the rules involving *-er* and *-ier* endings and provide a bank of commonly used words that require the use of *more*.

---

3 Understand

Review Ask students to help you make a list of ways in which geography helps the Pacific islands' economies and another list of ways in which geography hurts the economies. Compare lists.

Assess Have students write their responses to the Assessment questions in their notebooks. Ask them to explain whether they agree or disagree with the following statement: *For the Pacific islands, the past was easier than the present.*

Remediate If students struggle to appreciate the need for changes in many island economies, have them revisit the text to find examples of changes many islands are hoping to make in order to grow their economies. List these in the *Cause* column of a two-column table. Then ask students to predict the effects of these changes in the *Effect* column of the table.

Name _____ Class _____ Date _____

 myWorld Activity Support   **GDP Calculator**

How Much per Person?

Directions Complete the table below by calculating each nation's
Gross Domestic Product (GDP) per capita, or the GDP per person. To
do this, divide the nation's GDP by its population. Then answer the
questions that follow.

Nation	Population (2010)	GDP (2008)	GDP per capita	Total land area (square miles)
Federated States of Micronesia	111,000	$238,100,000		271
Fiji	854,000	$3,668,000,000		7,054
Kiribati	100,000	$608,000,000		313
Marshall Islands	63,000	$133,500,000		70
Palau	21,000	$164,000,000		177
Papua New Guinea	6,888,000	$13,042,000,000		174,850
Samoa	179,000	$1,100,000,000		1,133
Solomon Islands	536,000	$1,070,000,000		10,633
Tonga	104,000	$553,000,000		277
Vanuatu	246,000	$996,000,000		4,710

Source: United Nations Population Division, CIA World Factbook, International Monetary Fund

1. Which Pacific island has the highest GDP per capita?

   _____

2. Which Pacific island has the lowest GDP per capita?

   _____

3. What connection do you see between an island's area and
   its GDP per capita? Explain why you think this is so.

   _____

   _____

   _____

QUICK FACTS

Getting Creative Many Pacific islands have looked beyond traditional economic practices for economic development. For example, Kiribati attracts businesses and agencies that need locations to launch spacecraft and communicate with satellites. In Fiji, companies bottle and export the island's drinking water. This industry brings in hundreds of millions of dollars.

Using Natural Resources

- How is tourism an example of how Pacific islanders depend on natural resources to make a living? (People from all over the world travel to see the beaches and plant and animal life on the islands. These tourists contribute money to the local economy.)

Analyze Visuals Ask students to compare the economic activity shown in the photograph with the map on the next page.

- Do you think islands with metals like gold and other mineral resources automatically have strong economies? Explain. (No. I can see from the map that Papua New Guinea, despite having deposits of gold, does not have one of the highest GDP per capita rates.)

Case Study

The Economy of the Pacific Islands

Key Ideas
- Many Pacific islands have developing economies that depend on the use of natural resources.
- Pacific leaders are working to improve the region's economy and build new industries for the future.

Key Terms
- subsistence farming
- copra
- Pacific Islands Forum
- Pacific Island Countries Trade Agreement

 Visual Glossary

▼ Papua New Guinea gold miners

The economy of the Pacific islands has changed dramatically in recent years. Pacific islanders have worked hard to modernize their traditional economies. They seek to increase trade with other countries and to develop new industries. But many of the islands have small populations and very limited resources. They are located far from most customers. Pacific islanders have yet to fully overcome these challenges.

Using Natural Resources

For thousands of years, the people of the Pacific islands have used the region's natural resources to support themselves. Islanders have fished, hunted animals, and gathered fruits and nuts.

In recent decades, Pacific islanders have begun using the region's resources in new ways. Some islands have many mineral resources. (For example, Papua New Guinea has gold.) On these islands, mining for minerals is an important part of the economy. On other islands, cutting trees for timber is a major economic activity. Tourism is also important. Many tourists travel to the region because of its sandy beaches and clear blue waters. Its rich diversity of plant and animal life also attracts visitors.

Still, fishing and agriculture are the two most important economic activities for most islands. Many farmers practice **subsistence farming,** or farming with little left over to sell. Other farmers grow crops for export. Coffee, cocoa, squash, and **copra**—dried coconut meat—are common export crops.

Reading Check What are the most important economic activities in the Pacific islands?

READING CHECK Fishing and agriculture are the most important economic activities.

CORE CONCEPTS: TRADE

Review Core Concepts Lesson 5.5 before discussing the Pacific islands' need for regional and global trade. Discuss whether the location and physical geography of the islands are advantages or disadvantages, as well as why residents might want free trade among the islands. Have students point to locations in the Pacific region, where they would expect a general balance of imports and exports to be impossible.

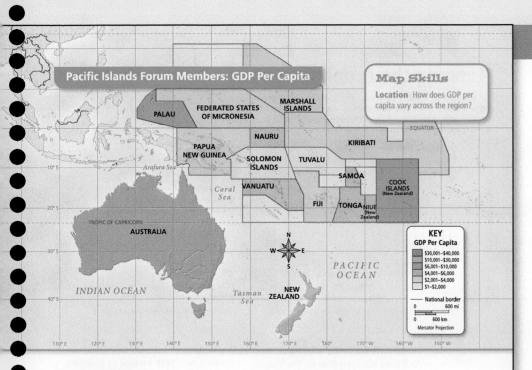

Pacific Islands Forum Members: GDP Per Capita

PALAU
FEDERATED STATES OF MICRONESIA
MARSHALL ISLANDS
NAURU
KIRIBATI
PAPUA NEW GUINEA
SOLOMON ISLANDS
TUVALU
VANUATU
SAMOA
COOK ISLANDS (New Zealand)
FIJI
TONGA
NIUE (New Zealand)
AUSTRALIA
NEW ZEALAND

Arafura Sea
Coral Sea
Tasman Sea
INDIAN OCEAN
PACIFIC OCEAN
EQUATOR
TROPIC OF CAPRICORN

Map Skills
Location How does GDP per capita vary across the region?

KEY
GDP Per Capita
$30,001–$40,000
$10,001–$30,000
$6,001–$10,000
$4,001–$6,000
$2,001–$4,000
$1–$2,000
National border
0   600 mi
0   600 km
Mercator Projection

Working Together

With their small sizes and limited resources and manufacturing, most Pacific islands import more goods than they export. In recent years, the region's economy has grown more slowly than the economies of many other regions.

Today many of the region's countries belong to the Pacific Islands Forum. The **Pacific Islands Forum** is an intergovernmental organization that aims to increase cooperation between and represent the interests of Pacific countries. Members discuss regional issues, such as education, tourism, and trade.

In recent years, the Forum has worked to increase economic growth in the region. Some proposals have involved making it easier for Pacific islanders to move from their homes to other islands in order to to find work.

Many Forum members have signed the **Pacific Island Countries Trade Agreement** (PICTA), an agreement intended to form a free-trade area among member nations. PICTA is designed to gradually reduce trade barriers in the region. Pacific islanders hope that making trade easier will improve the region's economies. They also hope that the agreement will help them increase trade with larger markets, such as Europe and the United States.

Reading Check How are the Pacific islands working to improve their economies?

READING CHECK To improve their economies, many islands are working together in the Pacific Islands Forum and trying to reduce trade barriers.

MAP SKILLS GDP per capita is highest in Australia and New Zealand. Besides Palau and the Cook Islands, where GDP is higher, and Solomon Islands and Tuvalu, where GDP is only $1 to $2,000, GDP per capita ranges from $2,001 to $6,000 across the other islands.

GUIDE ON THE SIDE

Map Skills Ask students to examine the map again, this time from north to south.

• What do Australia and New Zealand have in common? (They are the two countries in the region with the highest level of GDP per capita. They are also the two largest countries in terms of land area.)

Working Together

• **Sequence** How might PICTA help the Pacific islands trade with major markets all over the world? (If islands build up a strong trade network with each other, that network might make the region look like a stronger trade partner to other, bigger markets.)

• **Infer** What is the benefit of allowing islanders to move between islands for work? (Islands who need more workers get them, and workers who cannot find work on their home island can find it elsewhere and eventually bring money home. Both the home and adopted countries' economies would benefit.)

QUICK FACTS

Growth Rates Although economic growth among the Pacific islands is much slower than in other regions of the world, recent years have shown encouraging signs of progress. As the graph on this page illustrates, growth was at 2 to 3 percent during the late 1990s, dipping then jumping to 3.5 percent in 2004, and averaging 2.8 percent between 2005 and 2007. These increases are tied to improvements in macroeconomic policies, increased tourism and logging, as well as increased foreign aid.

Looking to the Future

- **Identify Details** What kind of aid do some poor islands need to survive? Where does this aid come from? (Some poor islands need foreign aid, money that comes from other countries, including the United States, Australia, and Japan.)

- **Connect** Explain how having access to the Internet could help a Pacific islands business, such as a small fishing company. (Sample: If the company had reliable Internet access, employees could regularly check on currents and weather reports, and research which fish were being purchased for the most money.)

Chart Skills Prompt students to compare the lines on the graph.

- According to the graph, what important event took place in 1997? (The Pacific islands' GDP growth was higher than the world growth rate.)

Planning the Economic Future

For years, the Pacific islands' economies have grown more slowly than the rest of the world's economy. Pacific leaders are working to improve education and build new industries for the future.

Pacific Islands and World: GDP Growth, 1995–2008

SOURCE: World Economic Outlook, 2008

■ Pacific Islands ■ World

▲ Government leaders seek to develop the region's economy.

Chart Skills

How does the rate of GDP growth in the Pacific islands compare to the world's GDP growth?

21st Century Learning

Looking to the Future

As Pacific islanders plan for the future, they hope to increase economic growth. Many also wish to reduce their reliance on foreign aid from Australia, the United States, Japan, and other nations. Today, a number of poor islands depend on this aid. For example, more than 20 percent of Kiribati's income comes from foreign aid.

Protecting the Environment Pacific economies often depend on the environment, for example, through fishing, tourism, or mining. As a result, protecting the environment is an important economic issue. In some areas, overfishing has reduced the supply of sea resources. Logging has caused deforestation and the near extinction of animal and plant species. Some of the beaches and coral reefs that attract tourists have been harmed by pollution.

But limiting activity that harms the environment may also affect economic growth. For example, limiting fishing in order to protect sea life also limits the amount of money that the region's people can make from fishing.

Working for Change Government leaders are seeking to replace traditional economic practices with new industries and new technologies. They are also trying to improve existing industries. For example, cellphones and better access to the Internet will improve communications and make business easier to conduct. Improving air transport will make it easier to ship goods and for tourists to visit the region.

CHART SKILLS 1. After lagging behind world GDP growth for years, GDP growth in the Pacific islands is now beginning to catch up to the world rate.

ASSESSMENT 1. They use natural resources for food, exports, and to attract tourists. **2.** Islanders hope to be able to work more cooperatively and replace some

READING CHECK If islanders are well educated and learn important skills as children, they will become productive workers who will help grow their country's economy.

ECONOMY

Mobile Phones and the Internet Many economists believe that getting more Pacific islanders connected by mobile phones and the Internet, while encouraging competition among service providers, will dramatically boost the regional economy. These scientists argue that tourists will be more likely to visit the islands if they can stay in touch with family and friends at home. Economists also see phone and Internet use as a way to stay in touch with expatriate islanders, cut costs on business communications, and take advantage of distance-learning opportunities.

Connectivity remains spotty. For example, in 2007, mobile-phone use rates were slightly more than 50 percent in Palau, at 30 percent in Samoa, but less than 10 percent in Micronesia, Papua New Guinea, Solomon Islands, Marshall Islands, and Kiribati.

▲ Tourism is a major part of the region's economy.

▲ A classroom in the Cook Islands

- **Summarize** What does Tuvalu's rental of its domain name demonstrate about the flexibity of some regional economies? (Some islands are thinking beyond natural resources and typical economic activities to make more money.)

- **Draw Conclusions** How do you think providing people with a modern, high-quality education might help solve some of the Pacific islands' environmental problems? (If children learn more about the dangerous effects some economic activities have on the environment, such as the impact of logging on endangered species, they might be more likely to avoid or help stop these activities when they are adults.)

The small nation of Tuvalu provides an example of a creative use of technology for economic growth. Tuvalu's national Internet domain name is ".tv." The country rents the use of this name to people and businesses interested in starting video- or entertainment-related Web sites. In 2006, Tuvalu earned more than $2 million from renting .tv—about 13 percent of its total GDP.

Technological improvements may only happen if islanders are able to improve their education and training. In some countries, children often end their schooling before graduating from high school. A number of governments and international organizations are working to provide education and training that will prepare residents for new economic activities. They hope that better education will lead to new opportunities.

Reading Check Why are educational issues a concern for the region's economic future?

Assessment

1. How do Pacific islanders use natural resources?

2. In what ways do people hope to change the region's economies?

3. How are Pacific islanders working together?

4. Why is environmental protection an important economic issue?

5. Why has the Pacific economy generally grown more slowly than the economy of the rest of the world?

traditional activities with newer, more modern industries. They also want to increase trade opportunities. **3.** They have formed the Pacific Islands Forum and PICTA to address regional issues. **4.** The environment provides Pacific islanders with much of their economic activity, so it must be protected. **5.** The region's economy has grown more slowly because the Pacific islands were long isolated from other economies, as well as from modern technologies and major trade markets.

Antarctica

OBJECTIVES

Students will know

- important dates and events in the history of exploration in Antarctica.
- the geographic characteristics that make Antarctica unique.

Students will be able to

- summarize Antarctica's physical geography, climate, and natural resources.
- ask questions to gain new insights into Antarctica.

SET EXPECTATIONS

In this section, students will

- read Antarctica.
- make inquiries of an Antarctic researcher.
- go On Assignment in Antarctica.

CORE CONCEPTS

You may wish to teach or reteach the following lessons from the Core Concepts Handbook:

- Understanding Maps, p. 10
- Temperature, p. 34
- Types of Climate, p. 40

KEY

Differentiated Instruction		English Language Instruction		
L1 Special Needs	**L2** Extra Support	**ELL** Beginner	**ELL** Early Intermediate	**ELL** Intermediate
L3 On-Level	**L4** Challenge	**ELL** Early Advanced	**ELL** Advanced	

1 Connect
Make learning meaningful

Make Connections Tell students to think of a time they took a trip to an unfamiliar place. Ask what they were most curious and nervous about. Have them magnify these feelings to fit a trip to a still mysterious continent. Ask, How do you think you would prepare for your trip? What unknown factor would most interest you?

L4 Challenge Show students a Southern Hemisphere projection that includes both Australia and Antarctica. Have them predict how the distance between the two affects the climate, geography, and population of Antarctica.

Activate Prior Knowledge Tell students to think about land use in regions about which they have already learned. Ask the class to come up with a Top Three list of what motivates people to use land, such as accessing natural resources, as well as what motivates them to not use it.

L2 Extra Support Use the map and information in Core Concepts 3.5 to have students predict climate conditions in Antarctica.

Prepare Follow the steps in the section **Preview.** Preteach the Key Terms. Then have students complete *Word Wise* in their **Student Journal** using in-text clues and the glossary for help.

2 Experience
Teach knowledge and skills

Read Use **Background** notes and **Guide on the Side** questions to model active reading. Have students use *Take Notes* in their **Student Journal** to summarize main ideas about Antarctica's geography. Have students complete *Summarize* on the **21st Century Online Tutor** and apply this skill to reading the section.

L2 Extra Support To motivate students to learn about Antarctica, read aloud *Enrichment: An Antarctic Explorer.* Pause to have students paraphrase descriptions in the excerpt.

ELL Intermediate Tell students to read Early Explorers in the **Online Student Edition** while listening to the accompanying audio. Ask them to orally sequence the information in three sentences, using *First, Next,* and *Finally*.

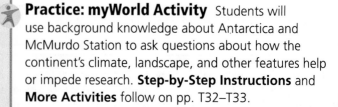

Practice: myWorld Activity Students will use background knowledge about Antarctica and McMurdo Station to ask questions about how the continent's climate, landscape, and other features help or impede research. **Step-by-Step Instructions** and **More Activities** follow on pp. T32–T33.

SECTION 4 RESOURCE GUIDE

FOR THE STUDENT

worldgeography.com Student Center
- Visual Glossary
- Active Atlas

Student Edition (print and online)
- Antarctica

Student Journal (print and online)
- Section 4 Word Wise
- Section 4 Take Notes

21st Century Learning Online Tutor
- Summarize
- Ask Questions

FOR THE TEACHER

worldgeography.com Teacher Center
- Online Lesson Planner
- Presentations for Projection
- SuccessTracker

ProGuide: Australia and the Pacific
- Lesson Plan, pp. T30–T31
- myWorld Activity Step-by-Step Instructions, p. T32
- Activity Support: Background Notes, p. T33
- myWorld Geography Enrichment, p. T34
- Section Quiz, p. T35

Accelerating the Progress of ELLs
- Reading Support Strategies, p. 42

3 Understand
Assess understanding

Review Review students' work in their **Student Journal**.

Assess Knowledge and Skills Use the Section Assessment and Section Quiz to check students' progress.

Assess Understanding Review students' responses to the Section Assessment Essential Question prompt.

Remediate Use these strategies to review and remediate.

If students struggle to . . .	Try these strategies.
Differentiate between related Key Terms, such as *ice sheet* and *glacier*	Make illustrated flashcards or word maps.
Summarize geographic causes and their effects	Have students practice summarizing using the **21st Century Online Tutor.**
Recognize the relationship between geographic accessibility and value	Discuss the role of location in determining how students judge a neighborhood's livability.

ELL Support

ELL Objective Students will be able to understand the significance of proper nouns in the reading.

Cultural Connections To connect to Antarctica's unique research opportunities, have students describe in their home language characteristics of the climate or landscape of a familiar country that foreigners often explore.

ELL Early Intermediate Content Tip Point out the initial capitalization in *Antarctic Treaty*. Review types of proper nouns and then ask students to find three other proper nouns in the section. Have students explain why each noun is proper and important to Antarctica.

ELL Activity Introduce the organizing principle of *Who, What, Where, When, Why,* and *How.* Have students make a chart with these headings to organize facts from *Activity Support: Background Notes.* Suggest that they use each heading as a jumping-off point for six questions to ask. **(Verbal)**

myWorld Activity | **Step-by-Step Instructions**

 30 min

Dear Antarctica

OBJECTIVES

Students will

- investigate life on an Antarctic research station.
- ask thoughtful questions about how conditions in Antarctica affect a scientist's style of living and research objectives.

LEARNING STYLE

- Verbal

21st Century Learning

- Ask Questions

MATERIALS

- Envelopes and postage
- Activity Support: Background Notes, p. T33

Activity Steps

1. Explain to students that they are going to have the opportunity to write to an actual scientist researching in Antarctica. First, they will read background information on the largest research station on the continent, McMurdo Station. Then they will use the information and data from Section 4 to write a letter you will help them send to the station.

2. Distribute copies of *Activity Support: Background Notes.* Allow students time to silently read the background information on Antarctica and then read it aloud to the class. Ask students to volunteer the information that surprises or interests them most.

   L2 Extra Support Ask students to highlight information from Section 4 that shows why Antarctica is so different from other continents. Work with students to sort these quotations into categories, such as Climate, Land, etc.

3. Review proper business-letter style and possible letter-writing prompts. Encourage students to write only one page and to check spelling and grammar. Also remind them that questions should focus on what makes working on Antarctica unique.

   ELL Intermediate Review the parts of an interrogative sentence, including the proper placement of the question mark. Explain why using *Why* and *How* will produce more than just a yes-or-no answer.

4. When students have finished their letters, have them share in pairs. Then copy and mail their letters to the following address during the Antarctic summer months (December–March): McMurdo Station, PSC 469 Box 700, APO AP 96599-1035. If students receive responses, post them to a classroom bulletin board or compile, copy, and distribute them for discussion and comparison.

More Activities From myWorld Teachers

Local Connections Have students speculate what effects the melting of Antarctica's ice cap could have on their location on Earth. Sort their ideas into short-term and long-term categories. **(Logical)**

Defend Post the following statement and have students take turns giving one-minute speeches explaining why they agree or disagree: *Antarctica's*

resources should be developed for the betterment of mankind. **(Verbal)**

Map the Sun Help students research how the tilt of the Earth and the path it takes around the sun affect Antarctica. Then have them annotate a world map with their findings, indicating how Antarctica's location connects to its climate and settlement. **(Visual)**

my worldgeography.com (Teacher Center) → Find additional resources in the online Teacher Center.

Name _____ Class _____ Date _____

myWorld Activity Support   **Background Notes**

Dear Antarctica

Directions Write a letter to a scientist working at McMurdo Station in Antarctica. First read the background information below. Then use the Letter Prompts to help you write your letter of educated questions for the scientist. Use separate sheets of paper.

Background Information McMurdo Station is the largest research station in Antarctica. Run by the United States, it was established in 1955 on a volcanic peninsula on the Ross Sea. This location is the southernmost point in Antarctica that can be reached by ship. During the continent's summer, snow disappears and temperatures rise, reaching an average of 26.6 degrees Fahrenheit in January. By August, winter has arrived with temperatures at an average of –18.4 degrees Fahrenheit. The number of scientists working at McMurdo changes with the temperature. In summer, there can be more than 1,000 people working there. In winter, this population drops to about 180 people.

McMurdo Station is the center of U.S. research in Antarctica. Researchers there study astronomy, biology, geology, and climate. They work to meet the goals of the United States Antarctic Program (USAP): to understand the climate, ecosystem, and other important geographic features of Antarctica. Scientists are only allowed to work on Antarctica when the USAP decides that their research projects cannot be conducted anywhere else in the world.

McMurdo Station provides some comforts, such as running water, a sewer system, electricity, and telephone and Internet service. The station also includes airplane runways on sea ice and shelf ice, as well as stores, a firehouse, and dormitories.

Letter Prompts As you write your letter, consider asking questions related to the following:
- the effect of Antarctica's climate on life and work
- research goals and expected results
- favorite and least favorite parts of living in Antarctica
- how Antarctica compares to other places in the world
- experience with Antarctica's ecosystem

Name _____ Class _____ Date _____

Enrichment: An Antarctic Explorer

Directions The selection below is from the journals of Thomas Orde-Lees, a ski and sled expert who accompanied Sir Ernest Shackleton on his 1914–1916 expedition to Antarctica. In the excerpt, Orde-Lees describes the unpredictability and beauty of the continent's ice and geography.

Read the selection. Then answer the questions that follow and complete the activity.

"The floe we were on appeared to be a piece of an old ice foot (ice formed during the winter and attached to the shore). It was very thick averaging 3 feet above water and probably 20 feet or so below, but in spite of this it proved to be very rotten being in process of disintegration by rotting and the action of the waves. . . .

"All night long the floe had been drifting towards the rest of the pack and before dawn, not only had it become part of the pack-edge but it was rapidly being included in the pack itself. By 7 A.M. we were so surrounded by broken pack that we were cut off from the edge of the pack by at least 100 yards of intervening ice. Our position began to look anything but satisfactory, but there was no alternative but to await events. There was now a huge swell running.

"The whole pack was [moving in waves] in a vast series of crests and troughs with a distance of over 100 yards between the summits of succeeding waves. Now we formed the top of the wave and the next minute we were in a deep valley with mighty [waves] rising some 12 feet or so on either side of us. It was a wonderfully impressive, awe-inspiring sight to thus see the whole ice covered ocean in motion.

"We waited and waited, hour by hour, watching the wonderful conflict of the elements, at times unmindful of our desperate position, spell-bound by the [impressive] majesty of the spectacle."

—Thomas Orde-Lees, April 11, 1916, journal entry

1. What happened to the ice floe on which the explorers were staying?

_____

2. What does Orde-Lees find amazing about his surroundings? Do you think you would feel the same way? Explain.

_____

3. Activity Imagine that you could interview Thomas Orde-Lees. Write five questions you would ask him about the expedition, such as his reaction to the climate or his expectations for Antarctica.

Name _____ Class _____ Date _____

Section Quiz

Directions Answer the following questions using what you learned in Section 4.

1. _____ How are icebergs related to glaciers?
   a. Icebergs are chunks of ice that break off of glaciers.
   b. Icebergs are larger than glaciers.
   c. Icebergs are slower moving than glaciers.
   d. Icebergs are seasonal but glaciers exist year-round.

2. _____ How does the ozone layer of the atmosphere affect Antarctica?
   a. It helps ultraviolet rays reach Antarctic ice.
   b. It helps freeze Antarctic ice.
   c. It filters out ultraviolet rays that can melt Antarctic ice.
   d. It is not related to Antarctica at all.

3. _____ How does pack ice change the geography of Antarctica in winter?
   a. It freezes on top of the continent's existing ice.
   b. It breaks off of glaciers in large, floating chunks.
   c. It floats on the surface of the continent's sea during winter.
   d. It produces new glaciers in the continent's valleys.

4. _____ What is the purpose of the Antarctic Treaty?
   a. to settle land disputes
   b. to preserve Antarctica for peaceful and scientific use
   c. to peacefully divide the continent among nations
   d. to declare the continent closed to expeditions

5. _____ What is the word used to describe a mass of compressed ice?
   a. pack ice
   b. ice sheet
   c. glacier
   d. Antarctica

6. Imagine that the Antarctic Treaty was never signed. List three ways in which Antarctica might be different today.

   1. _____
   2. _____
   3. _____

Antarctica

- Model preparing to read by previewing the Key Ideas, Key Terms, headings, visuals, and captions. Have students make predictions about what they will learn. For ELL support, post the prompt "I predict I will read about . . ."

- Preview and practice the reading skill Summarize by summarizing the main areas of science that someone might research in your community.

- Teach this section's high-use Academic Vocabulary using the table on the next page. Have students practice Academic Vocabulary and Key Terms by completing the *Word Wise* page in their **Student Journal.**

GUIDE ON THE SIDE

Physical Geography

- **Summarize** Describe Antarctica's landscape. (Antarctica is almost entirely covered by a sheet of ice.)

- **Compare and Contrast** Compare what you now know of Antarctica with North America. (Antarctica is farther south, is a smaller continent, and is mostly uninhabited.)

- **Predict** Why do you think Antarctica is the least populated continent? (It is too cold, dry, and windy. Most land is covered with ice, so it is impossible to grow food.)

 Reading Skill

Summarize While they read, have students practice this skill by completing the *Take Notes* graphic organizer in the **Student Journal.**

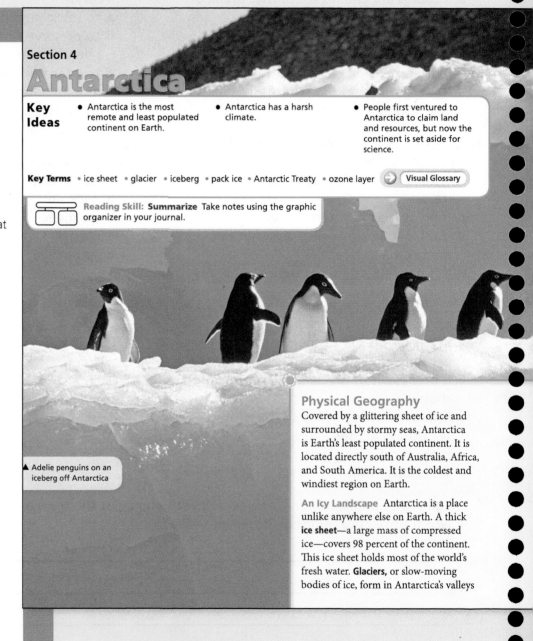

Section 4

Antarctica

Key Ideas
- Antarctica is the most remote and least populated continent on Earth.
- Antarctica has a harsh climate.
- People first ventured to Antarctica to claim land and resources, but now the continent is set aside for science.

Key Terms • ice sheet • glacier • iceberg • pack ice • Antarctic Treaty • ozone layer ⟳ Visual Glossary

Reading Skill: Summarize Take notes using the graphic organizer in your journal.

▲ Adelie penguins on an iceberg off Antarctica

Physical Geography

Covered by a glittering sheet of ice and surrounded by stormy seas, Antarctica is Earth's least populated continent. It is located directly south of Australia, Africa, and South America. It is the coldest and windiest region on Earth.

An Icy Landscape Antarctica is a place unlike anywhere else on Earth. A thick **ice sheet**—a large mass of compressed ice—covers 98 percent of the continent. This ice sheet holds most of the world's fresh water. **Glaciers,** or slow-moving bodies of ice, form in Antarctica's valleys

ACADEMIC VOCABULARY

High-Use Word	Definition and Sample Sentence
compound	*n.* something formed by two or more parts *The scientist mixed four chemicals to create a new compound.*

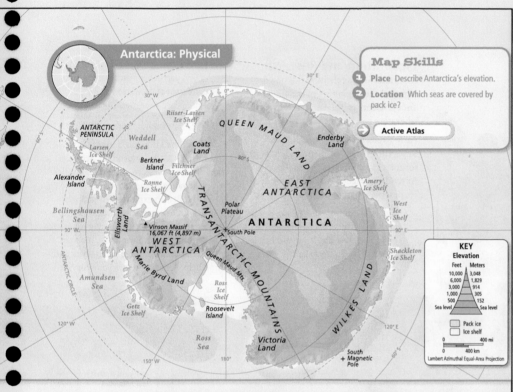

Antarctica: Physical

Map Skills

1 **Place** Describe Antarctica's elevation.
2 **Location** Which seas are covered by pack ice?

Active Atlas

KEY
Elevation
Feet	Meters
10,000	3,048
6,000	1,829
3,000	914
1,000	305
500	152
Sea level	Sea level

☐ Pack ice
☐ Ice shelf

0   400 mi
0   400 km
Lambert Azimuthal Equal-Area Projection

Map Skills Have students examine the map to identify geographic characteristics of West and East Antarctica.

- **Read Physical Maps** Describe the coast of Antarctica. (It is jagged and cut deeply in many places by the surrounding oceans.)

- **Identify Details** What landform acts as Antarctica's dividing line? (Transantarctic Mountains)

- **Draw Conclusions** Animals are more likely to be found in the oceans near Antarctica than on the continent itself. What does this tell you? (The ocean is a warmer and therefore easier living environment.)

and flow toward the coast. When glaciers reach the sea, the ice breaks off into **icebergs,** or large floating masses of ice.

In winter, the surface of the sea around Antarctica freezes, forming pack ice. **Pack ice** is seasonal ice that floats on the water rather than being attached to land.

The Transantarctic Mountains divide Antarctica into two regions, a large, flat area called East Antarctica and a smaller region called West Antarctica. At the tip of West Antarctica, the Antarctic Peninsula extends toward South America. The Transantarctic Mountains have glaciers and dry valleys free of snow and ice.

Climate, Life, and Resources Antarctica's interior is a high, dry plateau. It receives little precipitation, less than two inches per year. The snow that does fall does not melt. Instead, it piles up year after year, eventually turning into glacial ice.

Antarctica's mineral resources include coal and iron ore. Its harsh climate limits vegetation to simple plants such as algae and mosses. Penguins, seals, and other animals spend much of their time in the ocean. The seas are home to a variety of fish, whales, and other marine life.

Reading Check How do Antarctica's climate and landscape affect life there?

ANSWERS

 Active Atlas

Have students go to myworldgeography.com to further examine maps of Antarctica.

GEOGRAPHY

Antarctica's Seasons Due to the angle of Earth's axis and its revolution around the sun every 365 days, it seems that only two seasons occur in Antarctica. While four seasons technically exist (winter: late June through late September, spring: late September through late December, summer: late December through late March, and fall: late March through late June), the lack or abundance of sunlight and the extreme temperatures have led many scientists to describe the continent as experiencing only winter and summer. During the long winter, the sun is only seen for a few hours at a time, if at all. During the summer, there are days when the sun never fully sets and twilight is the darkest it gets. Temperatures can reach 36° F in summer, a stark contrast to the coldest winter days, when wind chill temperatures can drop to −130° F.

GUIDE ON THE SIDE

Exploration and Research

- **Analyze Cause and Effect** What dangers made early Antarctic exploration difficult? (blizzards, unpredictable ground conditions, ice that can destroy ships)

Analyze Visuals Ask students to trace the history of exploration shown in the three photographs.

- What does Antarctica offer to researchers that they cannot find anywhere else in the world? (almost nonexistent population, unique climate extremes, history preserved in ice)

myWorld Activity

Dear Antarctica Find Step-by-Step Instructions and an Activity Support on pp. T32–T33. **(Verbal)**

Exploration and Research

Antarctica was a relatively unknown region at the beginning of the 1900s. Today, scientists use Antarctica as a giant laboratory to examine the natural world.

Early Explorers In 1910, explorers Robert Scott and Roald Amundsen began separate expeditions to the South Pole. Amundsen reached it in December 1911. He described part of the journey:

> 66 Our walk across this frozen lake was not pleasant. The ground under our feet was evidently hollow, and it sounded as if we were walking on empty barrels. First a man fell through, then a couple of dogs … This part of our march was the most unpleasant of the whole trip. 99
> –Captain Roald Amundsen, *The South Pole: An Account of the Norwegian Antarctic Expedition in the Fram, 1910–1912*

Scott reached the Pole a month after Amundsen. On the return trip, Scott's team died in a blizzard. Still, their studies helped advance Antarctic science.

In 1915, British explorer Ernest Shackleton set out to cross Antarctica. His ship was destroyed by pack ice, forcing his team to live on an ice floe. Eventually, the men crossed the ocean in three small boats and found help. Amazingly, everyone survived.

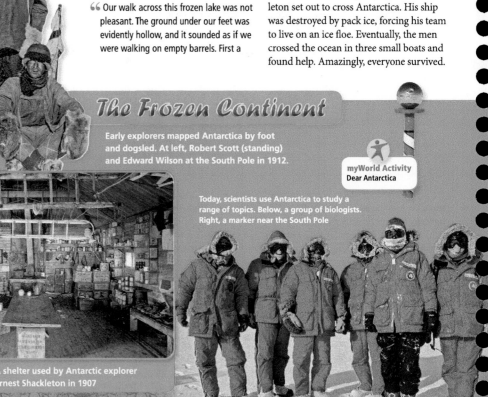

The Frozen Continent

Early explorers mapped Antarctica by foot and dogsled. At left, Robert Scott (standing) and Edward Wilson at the South Pole in 1912.

myWorld Activity
Dear Antarctica

Today, scientists use Antarctica to study a range of topics. Below, a group of biologists. Right, a marker near the South Pole

A shelter used by Antarctic explorer Ernest Shackleton in 1907

READING CHECK Today, people use Antarctica for research purposes.

SECTION 4 ASSESSMENT 1. The treaty preserves Antarctica for scientific use. **2.** Ice sheets are masses of compressed ice. Glaciers are slow-moving bodies of ice. Icebergs are chunks that break off of glaciers. Pack ice forms and floats on top of water. **3.** Antarctica's conditions are too cold and dry for long-term settlement. **4.** The climate makes it impossible for many species to survive there.

ECONOMY

Polar Tourism Given the difficulty involved in extracting Antarctica's natural resources, tourism may be the most valuable economic opportunity in the region. According to the International Association of Antarctica Tour Operators (IAATO), tourism to the icy continent has steadily increased since tourists first visited in 1970, rising from 6,704 visitors in the 1992–1993 season to 12,248 visitors in 2000–2001 to 45,213 in 2008–2009.

Tourism to the area is regulated by guidelines from groups associated with the Antarctic Treaty and IAATO, yet some governments claims that these guidelines are not doing enough to protect Antarctica's pristine environment from too many visitors and cruise-ship groundings. In 2009, U.S. President Barack Obama proposed amending the Antarctic Treaty to limit the number of ship landings and ensure one guide for every 20 persons.

GUIDE ON THE SIDE

Antarctica and Science Early explorers often claimed land in Antarctica. By the 1940s, these competing land claims led to international conflict. In 1959, twelve countries signed the **Antarctic Treaty,** an agreement that preserves Antarctica for peaceful and scientific use. Other protections were adopted in later years.

Today, Antarctica has no permanent human settlement. It does have several scientific research stations scattered across the continent. Scientists from a number of countries study topics such as oceans, glaciers, and climate.

Climate and the Ozone Layer To study climate, scientists drill deep into the ice sheet to gather ice samples. By examining the samples, they can learn more about the climate at the time when the ice was formed. By studying past climates, scientists hope to understand more about how climate might change in the future.

Scientists in Antarctica also study the ozone layer. The **ozone layer** is a layer of the atmosphere that filters out most of

the sun's harmful ultraviolet rays. Over time, the ozone layer over Antarctica has grown thinner. This area of reduced ozone, called the ozone hole, allows more ultraviolet radiation to reach Earth. A major cause of the hole in the ozone layer has been certain human-made chemical <u>compounds</u>. Today, most uses of these compounds have been banned. Scientists predict that the ozone layer will eventually recover if this ban is maintained.

compound, *n.,* something formed by two or more parts

Reading Check How do people use Antarctica today?

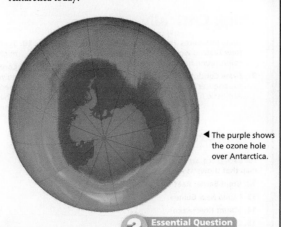

◀ The purple shows the ozone hole over Antarctica.

- **Synthesize** How can Antarctica's ice give scientists a better idea of what the world was like centuries ago? (When scientists drill to reach ice samples, they can access climate information from long ago.)

- **Infer** What is the danger of allowing more of the sun's rays to reach Antarctica? (The continent's ice could melt, which would drastically change the continent and eventually the world's climate and oceans.)

Section 4 Assessment

Key Terms

1. How does the Antarctic Treaty affect Antarctica?

2. Give short definitions of each of the following terms: ice sheet, glacier, iceberg, and pack ice.

Key Ideas

3. Why is Antarctica the least populated continent?

4. How does Antarctica's climate affect its environment?

5. Why are scientists interested in studying Antarctica?

Think Critically

6. **Draw Conclusions** How might its geography explain why Antarctica was not explored or settled until relatively recently?

7. **Synthesize** What challenges might Antarctica face in the future?

? **Essential Question**
What makes a nation?

8. Why have no nations formed in Antarctica?

ANSWERS

5. Scientists can use ice formed long ago to study past conditions. They can also learn about nature in its untouched form from the continent. 6. Antarctica was too difficult to travel to or to survive on until technology improved. 7. Antarctica might face the challenge of increased exposure to the sun's rays. 8. Sample: Antarctica's climate and environment make it very difficult to form settlements. Also, the Antarctic Treaty preserves the continent for peaceful and scientific use.

1. Islands are formed by volcanoes, where magma has been pushed to the surface at plate boundaries.

2. Humans settled in three waves of migration, moving from Southeast Asia to New Guinea and Australia; then to Micronesia and Melanesia; and then to Polynesia and south to New Zealand. Europeans arrived in the region during the late 1700s.

THINK CRITICALLY

8. Sample: The countries might be similar, since another European power might have seen the value of both regions; If European settlers had not arrived, the countries might have developed into nations run by indigenous peoples.

9. Sample: Explorers' reports of how harsh the geography and climate of Antarctica were may have convinced countries that the continent was better suited for research than colonization.

10. Sample: More people might move to the wetter coastal areas, raising the already high population density in those regions. Australia's economy might change as people find ways to replace the money they have lost from not being able to grow as many crops or raise as much livestock.

11. Sample: Nonnative species might compete with native species for space and resources, and they might harm native animals not used to eating those types of plants. Governments should try to ensure that native species have their own space to grow, and forbid people from introducing nonnative species in those areas.

3. drought, climate change, long-term effects of nuclear testing, rising sea levels

4. Whereas most people in Australia and New Zealand live in cities, the population of other islands is more rural and spread out.

5. Sample: Ethnocentrism is the belief that your culture or ethnic group is better than all others.

6. Sample: They are descended from the groups of people who lived in Australia and New Zealand when Europeans first arrived.

7. It preserves the continent for peaceful and scientific use only. It also specifically protects parts of the Antarctic environment.

Australia and the Pacific

Chapter Assessment

Key Terms and Ideas

1. **Describe** How does **plate tectonics** explain the creation of volcanic islands in the Pacific?
2. **Recall** How did people settle the Pacific region?
3. **Summarize** What environmental issues does the region face?
4. **Compare and Contrast** Describe population density in Australia, New Zealand, and the Pacific islands.

5. **Paraphrase** Explain **ethnocentrism** in your own words.
6. **Summarize** What do **Aborigines** and the **Maori** have in common?
7. **Recall** How does the **Antarctic Treaty** protect Antarctica?

Think Critically

8. **Draw Inferences** How do you think Australia and New Zealand would be different today if British colonization had never taken place?
9. **Draw Conclusions** How might early explorers' experiences have helped to inspire the Antarctic Treaty?

10. **Synthesize** If drought continues in Australia, how might its population and economy change?
11. **Core Concepts: Climates and Ecosystems** How do you think the introduction of nonnative plant species has affected the Pacific region's ecosystem? What do you think can be done to better protect native species?

Places to Know

For each place, write the letter from the map that shows its location.
12. Great Barrier Reef
13. Papua New Guinea
14. Mount Kosciuszko
15. Darling River
16. Southern Alps
17. Indian Ocean
18. **Estimate** Using the scale, estimate the distance between the northwest tip of Papua New Guinea and the Southern Alps.

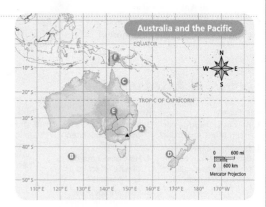

Australia and the Pacific

PLACES TO KNOW
12. C
13. F
14. A
15. E

16. D
17. B
18. about 30,000 miles (48,000 kilometers)

 **myWorld Chapter Activity**

Reporting Back: A Voyage to the Pacific Find Step-by-Step Instructions, Student Instructions and Rubric, and an Activity Support on pp. T5–T7. **(Verbal/ Visual)**

21st Century Learning

Search for Information on the Internet Students' reports should demonstrate an ability to locate, verify, and process information from various Web sites in original ways. If students need help with this skill, direct them to *Search for Information on the Internet* on the **21st Century Online Tutor.**

Online Assessment

Tailor review and assessment to each student's needs with an array of online assessments.
- Self-Test
- On Assignment Article or Slideshow
- Success Tracker

? Essential Question

What makes a nation?

Reporting Back: A Voyage to the Pacific Follow your teacher's instructions to investigate geographic features of Australia and New Zealand as a member of explorer James Cook's crew. Work with your team members to collect and organize information on your field of expertise. Then prepare a multimedia presentation on the region to present to the British king.

21st Century Learning

Search for Information on the Internet

Imagine that you work at a U.S. zoo planning an exhibit on Antarctic penguins, leopard seals, and other animals. Use the Internet to research how to create an accurate exhibit. Then use this information to write a brief report. Remember to consider the following:
- Antarctica's climate and landscape
- Antarctica's land and sea temperatures
- the needs of Antarctic animals

Document-Based Questions

 Success Tracker™
Online at myworldgeography.com

Use your knowledge of Australia and the Pacific and Documents A and B to answer Questions 1–3.

Document A

Internet Users	
Country	Users per 100 People
Australia	75.1
New Zealand	78.8
Papua New Guinea	1.8
Tonga	3.0
Vanuatu	3.5

SOURCE: United Nations Statistics Division

Document B

" I was definitely not told that I was Aboriginal. What [they] told us was that we had to be white. It was drummed into our heads that we were white … We were prisoners from [the moment] we were born."

—John, an Aboriginal man who was taken away from his family as a child in the 1940s

1. Examine Document A. What can you conclude about Pacific economies based on these data?

   A Australia and New Zealand are less developed than other countries in the region.

   B Australia and New Zealand are more developed than other countries in the region.

   C Countries in the region are equally developed.

   D Smaller countries are more developed than larger countries.

2. Read Document B. What does the quotation describe?

   A climate change

   B forced assimilation

   C migration

   D missionaries

3. **Writing Task** Do you think the situation described in Document B was common? Explain your answer.

WRITING TASK TIP

Outlining Essays Tell students that outlines can be used for everything from long essays to answers only a couple of paragraphs long. Also point out that as long as each item in an outline represents only one main idea or one supporting detail, the outline can be as long as students want. Explain that a long outline does not necessarily produce a long essay, since supporting details, and sometimes main ideas, can be combined in one paragraph. Remind students that subheadings should contain more specific information than headings.

DOCUMENT-BASED QUESTIONS

1. B

2. B

3. Students' answers, comprising of at least two paragraphs, should draw upon information about Australia's indigenous people from Sections 2 and 3. Students should mention the poor treatment of Aborigines by British settlers and white Australians and the general theories behind ethnocentrism and forced assimiliation.

HISTORY

The Aborigines The Aboriginal people of Australia originally migrated from Asia, beginning some 45,000 to 60,000 years ago. Scholars are not sure whether one or several waves of migration occurred. The Aborigines spread across the continent and inhabited all of it by about 35,000 years ago. By the time Europeans arrived in Australia, the Aborigines spoke some 200 different languages. They were organized into about 500 groups along linguistic and cultural lines rather than by territorial holdings. However, their group identities were not hard and fast. Much cultural diffusion took place, and groups built a complex network of relationships through barter, marriage, and shared religious observance.

GUIDE ON THE SIDE

21st Century Learning

Develop Cultural Awareness Ask, What are some of the categories that fall under the topic of culture? Students might name music, art, literature, television, movies, customs, or food. List their categories on the board. For each category, ask students to name famous individuals associated with that aspect of culture. For example, for movies they might name Steven Spielberg or George Lucas. Tell the class that they are going to research people who have contributed to the culture of Australia and the Pacific and choose one person to be the subject of a biography.

21st Century Learning   Develop Cultural Awareness

Meet the Islanders

Your Mission Working in groups, you will research the indigenous peoples of Australia, New Zealand, and the Pacific islands. Then you will choose a person from one of those groups, research his or her life, and develop a multimedia biography.

One memorable moment of the 2000 Olympic Games in Sydney, Australia, came when Cathy Freeman won the 400-meter race. She was the first person of Aboriginal descent to win an Olympic medal. She took her victory lap proudly waving both the Australian and Aboriginal flags.

Many indigenous groups are found in Australia, New Zealand, and the Pacific islands. The indigenous people of Australia are known as Aborigines. The Maori are the indigenous people of New Zealand. The Pacific islands have a variety of indigenous cultures.

MEET THE ISLANDERS RUBRIC
3. Every student in the group researched well-known people from their assigned indigenous group. All students took part in choosing the subject for the biography. The group researched the subject's family, childhood, adult life, achievements, and ethnic heritage. The group presented a multimedia biography that included a variety of materials including text, videos, music, photographs, and other visuals.

CULTURE

Polynesians The largest of the three Pacific Island groups is the Polynesians. Polynesia encompasses a large triangular region that extends from New Zealand in the west, to Easter Island in the east, and to the Hawaiian Islands in the north. Polynesians settled such a vast region by traveling from island to island in huge voyaging canoes. They navigated by using stick charts, grids made from bamboo sticks with shells to represent islands. The charts showed the islands in relation, not to each other, but to the prevailing winds and waves. By using such charts, Polynesians were able to travel safely across immense distances.

Go to myWorldGeography.com for help with this activity.

STEP 1

Choose a Subject.

Assign each person in your group to research one of these groups: Aborigines, Maori, and indigenous Pacific islanders. As you learn about these peoples, make a list of well-known or prominent individuals with that heritage. Try to include people from the arts, politics, sports, entertainment, science, and other fields. Share your findings and, as a group, choose one person to be the subject of your multimedia biography.

STEP 2

Research the Subject.

Do additional research on your subject's life and achievements. Divide up the tasks of finding out about the subject's family and childhood, adult life and achievements, historical events from his or her lifetime, and the customs and heritage of his or her ethnic group. Try to find lively details to enhance your presentation. Share your research with your group, and together decide what you will include in the biography.

STEP 3

Make a Presentation.

Plan and present a multimedia biography about your subject. Consider using written materials, photographs, videos, music, and other elements. Your biography should be thorough and focused. It should include interesting details as well as accurate facts. Your presentation to the class may take the form of a multimedia slideshow, a podcast, a radio broadcast, a documentary, or an interactive Web site.

2. The group listed a few people for each group. Most students helped choose a subject. The group researched some aspects of the subject's life. The multimedia biography included some of the following: text, videos, music, photographs, and other visuals.

1. The group listed a few people for some groups. Few students helped choose a subject. The group researched few aspects of the subject's life. The multimedia biography included two of the following: text, videos, music, photographs, and other visuals.

ANSWERS

Australia and the Pacific

See rubric on p. T6.

myWorld Chapter Activity: Reporting Back: A Voyage to the Pacific

Notes and Key Points from Activity Cards

General Information The route to the region includes a number of islands; the trip requires many crew members and plenty of food. If ships follow Cook's route, a trip to the region takes almost a year.

Cook's Journal Altitude varies, farming and cattle-raising are possible, and settlements could probably be established near major bodies of water. Long coasts offer many opportunities for sheltered harbors. There is good potential for agriculture.

People There are more indigenous people in Australia than in New Zealand, with more established land use in New Zealand. Settlers would have to learn to live with Aborigines and the Maori; settlers may need to study Aboriginal and Maori customs and ways of life in order to coexist peacefully.

Plants and Animals The region is home to many native species found nowhere else in the world, including plants with medicinal and practical use and some animals for hunting. Once settlers become more familiar with the native species, they can use these species for many purposes.

Climate Conditions are mild and wet in spots, and hot and dry in others. Settlement might be easier on the coasts.

Resources There is some fertile soil, as well as plenty of marine life and timber. Agriculture is possible in some parts of the region. Seafood and timber should help support new settlements.

Presentation Answers Presentations will vary. Students should use the information they have collected and organized to make a compelling, active, graphics-heavy presentation that also argues for or against eventual settlement in the region, citing how the advantages of the area do or do not outweigh the long travel time. Teams should highlight the challenges of settling land on which people already live, as well as dealing with the unknown in terms of farming, construction, and climate.

Section 1
Chapter Atlas

myWorld Activity: Travel Tips

Travel Guide Answers Answers will vary, but students should incorporate a number of facts from Section 1. Sample answer:

What kind of climate to expect The climate of the region varies. It can be very hot in the interior of Australia, but rainy along its eastern coast. While New Zealand is cooler than Australia, the other Pacific islands are typically hotter, with heavy precipitation.

What you can see and do Visit the banana farms on high Pacific islands and sunbathe on the sunny beaches in Micronesia. In Australia, dive on the coral reefs of the Great Barrier Reef and see Ayers Rock in the Outback. Climb volcanic peaks and discover native animals and plants in New Zealand.

How to avoid crowds Stay away from the eastern coast of Australia, especially Sydney and Melbourne. Try central Australia, New Zealand's South Island, or some of the lower-lying Pacific islands, which usually have small populations.

Items to pack Raincoat for visiting Australia's eastern coast, extra suitcase for bringing home gold and cacao souvenirs.

Enrichment: Kiwi: More Than Just a Bird

1. Sample: New Zealanders probably thought that a creature found only in their country was a good symbol for themselves.

2. Sample: They should keep people from trapping or killing kiwi and forbid construction near kiwi habitats.

3. Answers will vary, but students should create brochures that show the cause-and-effect relationship between some construction practices and kiwi habitat loss.

Section 1 Quiz

1. c **2.** b **3.** b **4.** b **5.** d
6. Sample answers in order of Climate, Physical Geography, Population, and Natural Resources:

Just Australia wet in north and east, dry overall; much dry land, deserts, fertile plains, coral reefs; majority on coast in cities; bauxite, lead, diamonds, coal, natural gas, pastureland, some fertile soil

Just Polynesia high temperatures, heavy precipitation; atolls, mountains; heavier population on higher islands; pastureland, fertile soil

Both Australia and Polynesia sometimes heavy precipitation; some fertile areas; big urban populations; some fertile soil, mineral resources

Section 2
History of Australia and the Pacific

myWorld Activity: Before and After Illustrations

Sample Before Illustration of nomadic Aborigines, as described in text, with caption *Aborigines were nomadic, moving together in small groups from place to place.* **Sample After** Illustration of a Western-style city, with caption *European settlers took control of much of the land Aborigines used, wanting to own it instead of use it collectively. They began changing the land to meet their own wants and needs.*

Enrichment: Cook and the Chronometer

1. Cook used the chronometer to plot his exact location while sailing. He was then able to draw accurate maps of the South Pacific.

2. Sample: The chronometer probably made many explorers feel much more confident about their travels. Also, they could now more accurately report back on their findings and direct others to the locations they had found.

3. Students' lists will vary, but should demonstrate five very clear differences between the old and new maps, such as discrepancies between physical locations, location names, and the size of oceans and islands.

Section 2 Quiz

1. b   **2.** a   **3.** c   **4.** d   **5.** c
6. Students' choice of events will vary. Samples: 40,000 years ago, The first people arrive in Australia and Melanesia. Late 1700s, British settlement of Australia begins. Today, Australia, New Zealand, and most Pacific islands are independent.

Primary Source: Aborigines Under British Rule

myWorld Activity: In Your Own Three Words

Samples: **Three words that describe Flinders Island** depressing, contagious, unfair **Three words that describe the Aboriginal Protection Act** strict, limiting, controlling **Three words that describe the needs of Aborigines in the 1800s** land, medicine, fairness **Three words that describe the needs of British settlers in the 1800s** land, money, control

Section 3
Australia and the Pacific Today

myWorld Activity: Take Action on the Pacific Environment

Answers in order of Issue, People Affected, Short-Term Effects, and Long-Term Effects:

Issue 1 Farmers, exporters. Some food may become more expensive. Agriculture might change as an industry.

Issue 2 Everyone, since nature benefits all. Some species will be affected. Entire species might disappear.

Issue 3 People living in low-lying areas, especially atolls. People might have to move temporarily when levels rise. Entire islands might have to be abandoned.

Issue 4 Fishermen/women, people who directly depend on fish for survival. Fish and the marine life that depends on them might become more scarce. The region's fishing industry might disappear, as well as some species of fish.

Sample Solution For Issue 4, I propose the following solution: Citizens and government should work together to set fishing limits that will prevent overfishing and help people in the fishing industry find other ways to make up lost income.

Enrichment: Disappearing Reefs

1. Sample: warmer and more acidic oceans, dynamite fishing, topsoil runoff

2. Humans depend on the reefs for food, income, and enjoyment. The reefs themselves can only survive if humans do not alter their environment.

3. Students' maps will vary, but at least three economic activities that might affect reefs should be marked, such as construction, farming, or logging.

Section 3 Quiz

1. a 2. b 3. a 4. d 5. c

6. Sample: A large number of cultures exist in the Pacific islands because the islands are typically far apart. Advanced transportation and communication methods did not exist until the past century, making it easier for cultures to develop on their own, mostly unaffected by other cultures in the world. As people learn more about each other, however, I think diversity will decrease. Cultures will begin changing and blending together.

Case Study: The Economy of the Pacific Islands

myWorld Activity: How Much per Person?

GDP Table Micronesia: $2,145; Fiji: $4,295; Kiribati: $6,080; Marshall Islands: $2,119; Palau: $7,810; Papua New Guinea: $1,893; Samoa: $6,145; Solomon Islands: $1,996; Tonga: $5,317; Vanuatu: $4,049

1. Palau

2. Papua New Guinea

3. Sample: Islands with less land area often have a lower GDP per capita. With less land area, there is less room to grow, make, and sell things. However, islands with large land area and many people, such as Papua New Guinea, can also have a relatively low GDP per capita.

Section 4 Antarctica

myWorld Activity: Dear Antarctica

Students' letters will vary. Students should use the prompts and other topics derived from the section text to write questions and some narrative. Letters should not simply be a list of questions; they should follow formal letter format. Questions might include, What have you found most difficult to adjust to while living in Antarctica? What do you hope your work will accomplish for Antarctica and the rest of the world? What animals have you seen in Antarctica that you have not seen in other places?

Enrichment: An Antarctic Explorer

1. It became part of a nearby ice pack.

2. Sample: Orde-Lees finds the ice-covered, moving ocean amazing. I might also find this amazing, but I would be scared that the piece of ice on which I was standing would not survive the waves.

3. Samples: What did you find most challenging about exploring Antarctica? If you returned to Antarctica, what would you do differently? How do you think Antarctica will or should be used in the future? What are Antarctica's biggest advantage and biggest disadvantage? What should the rest of the world keep in mind when they consider sending more expeditions to Antarctica?

Section 4 Quiz

1. a 2. c 3. c 4. b 5. b

6. Samples: People might have tried to extract natural resources, perhaps by drilling for oil. People might have tried to create settlements. Different countries might have claimed parts of the continent and then fought over ownership.

Acknowledgments

The people who made up the **myWorld Geography** team—representing composition services; core design, digital, and multimedia production services; digital product development; editorial; editorial services; materials management; and production management—are listed below.

Leann Davis Alspaugh, Sarah Aubry, Deanna Babikian, Paul Blankman, Alyssa Boehm, Peter Brooks, Susan Brorein, Megan Burnett, Todd Christy, Neville Cole, Bob Craton, Michael Di Maria, Glenn Diedrich, Frederick Fellows, Jorgensen Fernandez, Thomas Ferreira, Patricia Fromkin, Andrea Golden, Mary Ann Gundersen, Christopher Harris, Susan Hersch, Paul Hughes, Judie Jozokos, John Kingston, Kate Koch, Stephanie Krol, Karen Lepri, Ann-Michelle Levangie, Salena LiBritz, Courtney Markham, Constance J. McCarty, Anne McLaughlin, Rich McMahon, Mark O'Malley, Alison Muff, Jen Paley, Gabriela Perez Fiato, Judith Pinkham, Paul Ramos, Charlene Rimsa, Marcy Rose, Rashid Ross, Alexandra Sherman, Owen Shows, Melissa Shustyk, Jewel Simmons, Ted Smykal, Emily Soltanoff, Frank Tangredi, Simon Tuchman, Elizabeth Tustian, Merle Uuesoo, Alwyn Velasquez, Andrew White, Heather Wright

Maps
XNR Productions, Inc.

Illustration
Kerry Cashman, Marcos Chin, Dave Cockburn, Jeremy Mohler

Note: T page numbers below refer to teacher resource pages. Other page numbers refer to Eastern Hemisphere Student Edition pages.

Photography
TABLE OF CONTENTS: Pages vi–vii, All, Pearson Education, Inc.

AUSTRALIA AND THE PACIFIC REGIONAL OVERVIEW: Pages 718–723, **Bkgrnd sky,** ImageSource/Getty Images; **Page 719, M,** Pearson Education, Inc.; **Bkgrnd,** Peter Bush/Dorling Kindersley; **720, R,** Ross Armstrong/Alamy; **L,** Martin Horsky/Shutterstock; **721, T,** Chad Ehlers/Getty Images; **B,** Ian Cumming/ Getty Images; **722, RT,** Stephen Alvarez/Getty Images; **LB,** David Messent/ Photolibrary; **RB,** Paul Nevin/Photolibrary; **LT,** Ted Mead/Photolibrary; **723,** Pearson Education, Inc.

AUSTRALIA AND THE PACIFIC: PageS 724–727, **All,** Pearson Education, Inc.; **T12,** Dave King/Dorling Kindersley; **728, Inset,** Rob Howard/Corbis;

Bkgrnd, Craig Tuttle/Corbis; **730,** George Steinmetz/Corbis; **732, L,** Liv Falvey/ Shutterstock; **R,** Tap10/Shutterstock; **Bkgrnd,** Thomas Schmitt/Getty Images; **M,** Dave Watts/naturepl.com; **733, L,** David Messent/Photolibrary; **R,** Peter Wey/Shutterstock; **M,** Ralph Loesche/Shutterstock; **734,** Craig Mayhew (NASA/ GSFC) and Robert Simmon (NASA/GSFC); **735,** George Steinmetz/Corbis; **T18,** Judith Miller/Branksome Antiques/Dorling Kindersley; **736,** Alexander Turnbull Library, Wellington, N.Z. Ref. G-516; **738, L,** *Portrait of Captain Cook* (c. 1800) Copy of portrait in the National Maritime Museum, Greenwich, England, after Sir Nathaniel Dance-Holland. National Library of Australia, Canberra, Australia/The Bridgeman Art Library; **Bkgrnd,** Erich Lessing/Art Resource, NY; **R,** *The Harbour at Anamooka* (about 1820s–1830s), plate 82 from *Le Costume Ancien et Moderne* by Jules Ferrario. Color lithograph. Private Collection/The Stapleton Collection/The Bridgeman Art Library International; **739, L,** Cannon Collection/Australian Picture Library/Corbis; **Bkgrnd,** Lawrence Manning/ Corbis; **R,** Mark Baker/AP Photo; **740,** *Mssrs. White, Harris, and Laing With a Party of Soldiers Visiting Botany Bay Colebee at that Place When Wounded near Botany Bay* (c. 1790), Port Jackson Painter. Watercolor on paper. British Museum, London, UK/The Bridgeman Art Library International; **B,** The Print Collector/age Fotostock; **741, T,** Cannon Collection/Australian Picture Library/ Corbis; **B,** Oliver Gerhard/age Fotostock; **742,** Barry Lewis/Corbis; **743, R,** Pearson Education, Inc.; **LM,** Bob Krist/Corbis; **RM,** James Davis Photography/ Alamy; **L,** Penny Tweedie/Corbis; **744, LT,** Rob Griffith/epa/Corbis; **RB,** Palani Mohan/AP Photo/SMH; **LB,** Jonathan Marks/Corbis; **745,** Bruce Martin/ Alamy; **746, RB,** Ashley Cooper/Corbis; **LB,** Richard Vogel/AP Photo; **T,** Seth Resnick/Science Faction/Corbis; **M,** Ashley Cooper/Corbis; **748,** Neil Duncan/ Photolibrary; **750, L,** dpaint/Shutterstock; **R,** Chris Skelton/Reuters; **751, R,** Jeremy Hoare/Alamy; **L,** Reinhard Dirscherl/age Fotostock; **752,** Sea World of California/Corbis; **754, RT,** Courtesy: Anthony Gibson/National Science Foundation; **LB,** Galen Rowell/Corbis; **LT,** Bettmann/Corbis; **RB,** Galen Rowell/ Corbis; **755,** NASA.

AUSTRALIA AND THE PACIFIC UNIT CLOSER: Page 758, **L,** R McKown/ Shutterstock; **758–759, All,** Shutterstock.

Note: Every effort has been made to locate the copyright owner of material reproduced in this publication. Omissions brought to our attention will be corrected in subsequent editions.